F
R I V I E R A

PATRICK DELAFORCE

HarperCollins*Publishers*

YOUR COLLINS TRAVELLER

Your Collins Traveller Guide will help you find your way around your chosen destination quickly and easily. It is colour-coded for easy reference:

The blue section answers the question 'I would like to see or do something: where do I go and what do I see when I get there?' Within each topic you will find:

- A selection of the best examples on offer.
- How to get there, costs and opening hours for each entry.
- The outstanding features of each entry.
- A simplified map, with each entry plotted and the nearest landmark or transport access.

The red section is a lively and informative gazetteer. It offers:

- Essential facts about the main places and cultural items.
  What is La Bastille? Who was Michelangelo? Where is Delphi?
- Practical and invaluable travel information.
  Everything you need to know to help you enjoy yourself and get the most out of your time away, from Accommodation through Baby-sitters, Car Hire, Food, Health, Money, Newspapers, Taxis and Telephones to Youth Hostels.

Cross-references:

Type in small capitals – CHURCHES – tells you that more information on an item is available within the topic on churches.

A-Z after an item tells you that more information is available within the gazetteer. Simply look under the appropriate name.

A name in bold – **Holy Cathedral** – also tells you that more information on an item is available in the gazetteer – again simply look up the name.

CONTENTS

CONTENTS

RED SECTION

INTRODUCTION

Nearly a century ago, Queen Victoria visited, and approved of, the region known as the French Riviera. The area between Toulon and Bandol to the west and Menton to the east, including St. Tropez, Antibes, Cannes, Nice and Monaco, has since become the most glamorous holiday resort in the world.

Even now, despite overbuilding and the crowded corniches and beaches in high season, it remains the Côte d'Azur, the Blue Coast, made known to the outside world in 1887 by the French author and poet Stephen Liégard. It was the gorgeous range of colours – the red rocks, the dazzling range of blues of sky and sea, the greens of olive, palm and cypress trees – that brought the Impressionist painters to this Mediterranean coast: Renoir to Cagnes, Monet to Antibes, Berthe Morisot, Matisse and Dufy to Nice, and Signac's 'school' at St. Tropez. They all came, attracted by the variety of subjects, the clear light, the superb equable climate and the friendly atmosphere.

Many people think of the Riviera as being a glittering, sophisticated coastal strip of a score of resort towns with their attendant marinas – which it is – but they forget the charm of the hinterland and the 50 charming hill towns with their medieval streets, ramparts and churches. They are mostly within an hour's drive of the coast and make a happy contrast to its pressures (try driving on the corniches in the four daily rush hours!). Although eight million tourists, half of them French, annually visit the Riviera, mostly in midsummer, and some resorts become distinctly overcrowded, most of the towns absorb the influx with relative ease.

The Greeks established trading posts 2500 years ago at Hyères, St. Tropez, Antibes, Nice and Monaco, followed by the Romans. The area which covers the departments of Alpes-Maritimes and Var has known many 'foreign' visitors, from Saracens and Visigoths, Turks and Austrians, to Italians (Genoese in particular), North Africans, Germans and Britons. Apart from a little episode in 1793 when the British navy briefly besieged Toulon, the British have in the main made significant and peaceful contributions to the prosperity of the French Riviera.

Casino de Monte-Carlo

Nice has been a seaside resort since the Scottish novelist Tobias
Smollett made it popular in the 1760s. As a result, the Cavendish family
and the Duke of York soon patronized the town, and the English com-
munity, led by the Duke of Gloucester, built the suburbs of Lympia in
the east and Villanuova (Newborough) in the west. The failure of the
vital orange crop around Nice in 1849 convinced the local English
parson to persuade his large congregation to fund a massive building
programme, which resulted in the magnificent Promenade des Anglais,
one of the most attractive boulevards in the world. There were one
hundred English families in Nice in 1815, but just 40 years later there
were over eight hundred.

In 1834 Henry Lord Brougham and his daughter Eleonore put Cannes
on the map when he purchased land and a villa, wintered there and
persuaded the English gentry to do the same over the next 34 years.
When Stephen Liégard wrote his book in 1887, 23 years after the rail-

way was opened, he noted no less than 18 princes or grand dukes on this 'Côte d'Azur'. But it was Queen Victoria, who wintered and sketched in Nice from 1895-99, who gave the ultimate stamp of approval to this playground of the international set. Hotels called Victoria, Balmoral and Regina sprang up along the coast. Her rapscallion son, the Prince of Wales, later King Edward VII, however, had different tastes and tactfully enjoyed them at neighbouring Cannes. He brought his yacht *Britannia* to the harbour, stayed with the Cercle Nautique, gambled, drank and ate too much! In 1889 he took part in the Bataille des Fleurs and also visited Villefranche-sur-Mer, Monaco and Menton. The British royal family had finally and firmly put the French Riviera on the map. The crowned heads of Europe, including a tsar or two, followed its lead, came, saw and approved. Well might F. Scott Fitzgerald write, 'The resplendent names – Cannes, Nice, Monte-Carlo – begin to glow through their torpid camouflage, whispering of old kings come here to dine or die, of rajahs tossing Buddha's eyes to English ballerinas, of Russian princes turning the weeks into Baltic twilights in the lost caviare days.'

The slightly raffish reputation of the Riviera hinged for many years on the gamblers at the casinos. 'The Man who broke the Bank at Monte-Carlo' was a song that endeared itself to punters everywhere. Rich foreigners came with their mistresses to gamble at chemin de fer – initially from the 1860s at Monte-Carlo, and later at other resorts including Nice, Juan-les-Pins and Menton.

Since the time of the first visitors on the Grand Tour en route for the antiquities of Rome, the Riviera was considered to be a marvellous resort in which to winter. The summer was considered too hot for northern skins. Not even when Tobias Smollett extolled the therapeutic values of sea bathing in the late 18thC did the habit catch on. It was as late as 1928 that a Niçois restaurateur called Edouard Baudoin finally turned the tide. He bought the casino at Juan-les-Pins, 'built' a new beach, as well as a new restaurant, produced *les spectacles* and attracted the trendsetters for the summer season.

F. Scott Fitzgerald's *Tender is the Night*, published in 1934, persuaded the Anglo-Saxons of the power of 'the diffuse magic of the hot sweet south'. All the famous Hollywood stars took villas and half a dozen superb colour films of the Riviera were made with Rita Hayworth, Betty Grable, Errol Flynn, Gregory Peck and the beautiful young woman who became Princess Grace (née Kelly) of Monaco. Brigitte Bardot and her

glamorous film star friends 'launched' St. Tropez, and the modern painters (Picasso, Marc Chagall, Fernand Léger and Vaserély) came to live and paint in the region. Somerset Maugham, Graham Greene, Colette, Katherine Mansfield, Anthony Burgess and Dirk Bogarde have also added their lustre to the literary scene, using the local ambience for background material.

The glitter of casinos, grand hotels and restaurants continues to attract the international tycoons, their wives and mistresses, while the gorgeous flowers that abound along the coast are the inspiration and raw materials for the famous perfumes of Grasse, which the selfsame people delight in wearing. The sea sparkles and the blue skies (giving 300 days of sunshine each year) are tempered by the Mediterranean zephyrs. The beaches stretch for 50 km, some sand, some shingle, and there are nearly 40 yacht marinas.

The Riviera has a reputation for being expensive. It is true that you can spend a fortune at the Eden Roc, Hermitage or Negresco hotels. However, in Nice and Toulon there are scores of modest hotels and restaurants which are less expensive than their counterparts in the UK or US, and there are restaurants in Monaco-Ville, Menton and Villefranche-sur-Mer where a prix-fixe three-course meal costs a ridiculously small amount.

The Riviera also has a reputation for having a noisy, couldn't-care-less, hedonistic atmosphere. This may be true in Juan-les-Pins or St. Tropez but the region is nevertheless a powerhouse of art. There are 70 museums of great note, including Fondation Maeght in St. Paul-de-Vence; Beaux-Arts, Matisse and Chagall in Nice; Picasso at Antibes; Renoir at Cagnes; Léger at Biot; and Cocteau at Menton. There are also opera houses in Nice, Toulon and Monte-Carlo, and cultural activities throughout the year. The *vieilles villes* are still as picturesque now as they were centuries ago, and you will find interesting Roman antiquities at Fréjus and Cimiez (Nice), but apart from some baroque churches at Menton, Nice and Sospel, there are few major buildings of architectural significance.

The best of French-Provençal and Italian cuisines blend happily all along the coast, using a wide variety of sea and shellfish cooked with incomparable herbs and spices. A visit to any town or village market will introduce you to the culinary delights to come – an overwhelming range of colours and smells, with olives, olive oil and garlic in frequent use. Another pleasant surprise is that there are three local wines well worth seeking out, from the vineyards of Bandol, St. Tropez and Bellet (Nice).

Midsummer is chaotic, with crowds of visitors and many of the 500 annual artistic events and 20 international festivals falling in that period, but try, if you can, to time your visit for spring (the Carnival and Bataille des Fleurs in Nice, Menton and Grasse take place around Easter), early summer or autumn. In fact you can ski for most of the year in the 17 resorts inland from Nice and Menton. But whenever you go – not if, when – you will find the French Riviera irresistible. Judge for yourself whether the 'caviare days' are lost for ever in this blue lotus land.

VIEILLE VILLE Between Pl. du Général de Gaulle and the sea.
*The old town was once ruled by the Grimaldi (see **A-Z**). Narrow streets
such as rue Sade, Haut Castellet, rue James Close, cours Masséna and Pl.
Nationale are full of shops, cafés, bistros, galleries and small restaurants.*

CATHÉDRALE DE L'IMMACULÉE CONCEPTION
Ave Amiral de Grasse.
❏ 0900-1200, 1400-1900. ❏ Free.
*12th-17thC building on the site of a Roman temple, with a belfry,
notable Bréa altarpiece and art treasures.*

CHÂTEAU GRIMALDI & MUSÉE PICASSO
Ave Amiral de Grasse.
❏ 1000-1200, 1500-1830 Wed.-Mon. ❏ Combined ticket 25F.
*The castle is 12thC, but was rebuilt in the 16thC. There are pleasant bat-
tlement walks. The museum contains works by Picasso (see **A-Z**), and
his studio. Note his splendid ceramics and mythological paintings. The
Nicholas de Staël and archaeological collections are on the ground floor.*

MUSÉE ARCHÉOLOGIQUE Ave Amiral de Grasse.
❏ 1000-1200, 1500-1830 Wed.-Mon. ❏ 10F.
*In a Vauban fort are objects from Antibes' 4000 years of history; pottery,
urns, money, and artefacts from Etruscan, Greek and Roman ships.*

PORT VAUBAN & FORT CARRÉ
*The attractive port is full of pleasure boats, and from the 16thC Fort
Carré there are views of Cagnes-sur-Mer and Nice.*

CAP D'ANTIBES 2.5 km south of Antibes.
*A beautiful promontory with cliff-top walks. See the Musée Naval et
Napoléonien (1000-1200, 1500-1830 Wed.-Mon.; 15F), Jardin Thuret
(0830-1800 Mon.-Fri.) and Sanctuaire de la Garoupe (sailors' church).*

ZOO MARIN (MARINELAND) La Brague, 3 km north of Antibes.
❏ 0900-1800. ❏ 80F, child 40F.
Aquarium with dolphins, penguins, sea-lions, seals, whales, etc.

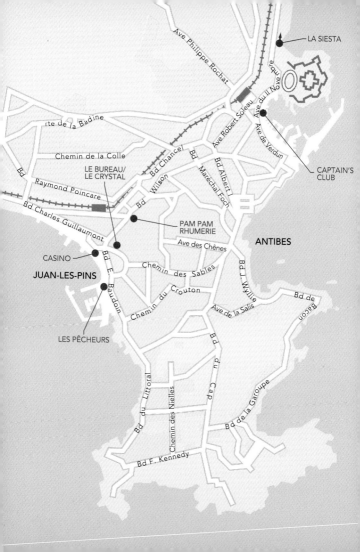

CAPTAIN'S CLUB 15 Ave du 11 Novembre, Antibes.
❑ 1900-0200.
An intimate pub serving delicious cocktails, which is part of Le Yacht restaurant and Hôtel Bellevue, and overlooks the port.

CASINO Ave Georges Gallice, Juan-les-Pins.
❑ Gaming rooms from 1800. Cinema and shows 2000-0400.
❑ Gaming rooms free.
A sophisticated cabaret plus dancing till dawn and games of chance.

LE BUREAU Ave Georges Gallice, Juan-les-Pins.
❑ 2300-0500. ❑ Entry and first drink 100F.
Smart 'in' disco for the young, with popular disc jockey called Alexandre, requiring tenue correcte de rigueur, i.e. smart dress. Live shows are held at weekends.

LE CRYSTAL Ave Georges Gallice, Juan-les-Pins.
❑ 2300-0400.
A chic disco for the young at heart. Cocktails are served on the terrace and there are 55 different beers to choose from.

LES PÊCHEURS Port Gallice, Juan-les-Pins.
❑ 2300-0500 June-Sep. ❑ Entry and first drink 80F.
Crowded fashionable nightclub with maritime décor and a brash and swinging clientele.

PAM PAM RHUMERIE 137 Bd Wilson, Juan-les-Pins.
❑ 1400-0500 mid Mar.-Oct.
Polynesian décor with tropical plants, woodcarvings and rattan furniture. Listen and dance to Brazilian, rock and reggae live bands in this noisy, exotic venue. Serves moderately-priced rum-based drinks.

LA SIESTA La Brague, rte du Bord de Mer, 3 km north of Antibes.
❑ 2030-0600 June-mid Sep. ❑ Entry and first drink 150F.
A large restaurant-casino with seven dance floors, and waterfalls lit by dramatic flaming torches. There is also roulette if you tire of the dancing.

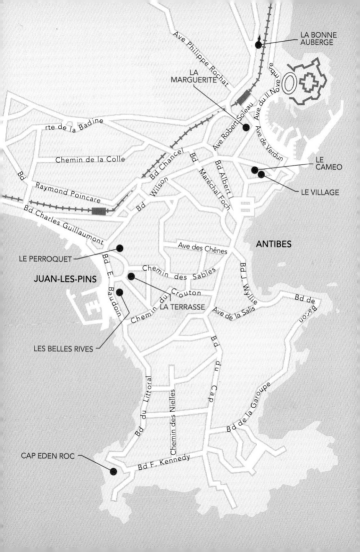

LA BONNE
AUBERGE

LA
MARGUERITE

Ave Philippe Rochat

Ave du 11 Novembre

LE
CAMEO

LE VILLAGE

rte de la Badine

Ave Robert Soleau

Ave de Verdun

Chemin de la Colle

Bd Chancel

Bd Albert I

Bd Maréchal Foch

Bd Wilson

Raymond Poincare

Bd Charles Guillaumont

Ave des Chênes

ANTIBES

LE PERROQUET

Bd E. Baudoin

JUAN-LES-PINS

Chemin des Sables

Bd J. Wyllie

Bd de Bacon

Crouton

LA TERRASSE

Ave de la Salis

Chemin du

LES BELLES RIVES

Bd du Cap

Bd de la Garoupe

Bd du Littoral

Chemin des Nielles

CAP EDEN ROC

Bd F. Kennedy

Restaurants

LA MARGUERITE 11 rue Sadi Carnot, Antibes.
❑ 1200-1430 Tue.-Sun., 1945-2130 Tue.-Sat. Closed April, May & Oct.
❑ Expensive.
Small restaurant with a good reputation. Try pintade à la mangue fraîche *(guinea fowl with mango) and* ragoût de coquilles *(shellfish stew).*

LA TERRASSE Hôtel Juana, Ave Georges Gallice, Juan-les-Pins.
❑ 1200-1500, 2000-2200. Closed lunch July-Sep. & mid Oct.-Easter.
❑ Expensive.
Inventive Provençal dishes, including rouget de roche à la vapeur de fenouil *(red mullet with steamed fennel). A top-ranking restaurant.*

LES BELLES RIVES Bd E. Baudoin, Juan-les-Pins.
❑ 1200-1415, 1930-2115. Closed mid Oct.-Easter. ❑ Expensive.
Terrace views of the sea, and classic Riviera cuisine and wines.

CAP EDEN ROC Bd F. Kennedy, Cap d'Antibes.
❑ 1200-1500, 2000-2245. Closed Nov.-Mar. ❑ Expensive.
One of the best hotel-restaurants on the Riviera. Superb cuisine.

LA BONNE AUBERGE La Brague, 3 km north of Antibes.
❑ 1200-1445, 2000-2200. Closed Nov.-mid Dec. ❑ Expensive.
Pink auberge in an indifferent location serving superb nouvelle cuisine.

LE CAMEO Pl. Nationale, Antibes.
❑ 1200-1415, 1900-2200. Closed Jan. & Feb. ❑ Moderate.
Family-run pension with a bar and restaurant, which is popular with locals. Also has a large terrace. Try the bouillabaisse.

LE VILLAGE 31 rue James Close, Antibes.
❑ 1200-1430, 2000-2300 Fri.-Wed. ❑ Moderate.
Good basic Provençal cooking. No frills and rustic décor.

LE PERROQUET Ave Georges Gallice, Juan-les-Pins.
❑ 1200-1430, 1945-2130. Closed Nov.-mid Jan. ❑ Moderate.
Good fish and shellfish dishes with Côtes de Provence wines.

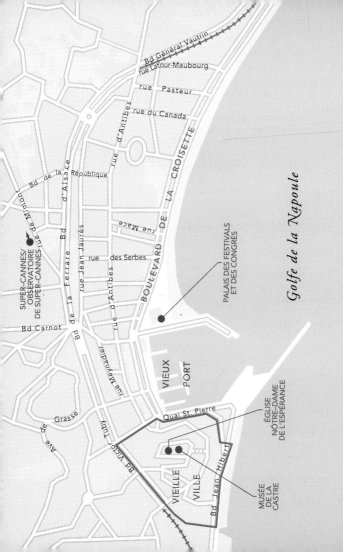

Bd Général Vautrin

rue Latour-Maubourg

rue Pasteur

rue du Canada

rue d'Antibes

Bd de la République

rue Macé

rue des Serbes

SUPER-CANNES/
OBSERVATOIRE
DE SUPER-CANNES

Bd Carnot

Bd de la Ferrare

rue Jean Jaurès

rue d'Antibes

rue Meynadier

Ave de Grasse

Bd Victor Tuby

Quai St. Pierre

VIEUX PORT

Bd Jean Hibert

VIEILLE VILLE

BOULEVARD DE LA CROISETTE

PALAIS DES FESTIVALS
ET DES CONGRÈS

ÉGLISE
NOTRE-DAME
DE L'ESPÉRANCE

MUSÉE
DE LA
CASTRE

Golfe de la Napoule

BOULEVARD DE LA CROISETTE

Famous, elegant, 3 km-long promenade with sandy beaches, palms, gardens, luxury hotels, boutiques, restaurants – and traffic. At the west end are the Vieux Port, Palais des Festivals et des Congrès and Casino Municipal. At the east end is Pointe de la Croisette with beaches, two marinas and superb views of Cap d'Antibes.

PALAIS DES FESTIVALS ET DES CONGRÈS

West end of Bd de la Croisette.
❑ Guided tours 1430-1700 Wed. (Nov.-June). ❑ Free entry.
Huge modern complex with a casino, tourist office and theatre, overlooking the Golfe de la Napoule and set in the President Georges Pompidou gardens beside the port.

VIEILLE VILLE (LE SUQUET) West of the Vieux Port.

On the hill above the Vieux Port are the Tour Sarrazine, 12thC Chapelle St. Anne, Église Nôtre-Dame de l'Espérance and Musée de la Castre. The Marché Forville and vaulted alleyways are very picturesque. Also see the 12thC Tour Mont Chevalier (1000-1200, 1400-1800 Wed.-Mon.; 10F).

ÉGLISE NÔTRE-DAME DE L'ESPÉRANCE Le Suquet.

❑ 0800-1200, 1500-1900.
16th-17thC church of Our Lady of Hope. The only 'old' church in Cannes. Concerts of musique sacrée are held throughout the year.

MUSÉE DE LA CASTRE Le Suquet.

❑ 1000-1200, 1400-1800 Wed.-Mon. ❑ 10F, Sun. & Wed. free.
The only museum in Cannes, with antiquities, artefacts, Egyptian mummies, Chinese porcelain, armour, vases, Etruscan urns, Persian portraits and a Mediterranean archaeological collection. Marvellous hotchpotch!

VIEUX PORT

*Crammed full of smart yachts and fishing boats. Cruise liners berth in the roadstead and ferries leave the gare maritime for excursions to the Îles de Lérins (see **Islands**). Picturesque houses painted in Provençal colours, and cafés, bistros and restaurants surround the port on three sides.*

SUPER-CANNES

The name given to the belle époque suburb inland from Pointe de la Croisette. Along La Californie are scores of opulent houses with towers, crenellations, tropical gardens, marble staircases, streams and fountains. See chateaux St. Georges and Scott, and villas Alexandre, Camille-Amélie, Champfleuri and Yakimour.

OBSERVATOIRE DE SUPER-CANNES 5 km northeast of
Cannes via the D 803.
❏ 0930-1800. ❏ 16F.
An observatory on La Californie hill which can only be reached by lift, from where there are fine panoramic views across the Mediterranean towards Corsica.

Bd Général Vautrin

rue Latour-Maubourg

PALM BEACH CASINO/
WHISKY À GOGO

rue Pasteur

rue du Canada

CARLTON
CASINO
CLUB

rue d'Antibes

rue de la Croisette

République

STUDIO
CIRCUS

Bd de la Alsace

Bd d'Alsace

rue de Mimon

rue Macé

Bd

rue Jean Jaurès

rue de

LE JANE'S

des Serbes

CASINO
LES FLEURS

rue d'Antibes

Bd

Bd Carnot

Bd de la Ferrare

LE CASINO
MUNICIPAL

RAGTIME

rue Meynadier

Ave de Grasse

Bd Victor Tuby

Quai St. Pierre

Bd Jean Hibert

Golfe de la Napoule

LE CASINO MUNICIPAL Bd de la Croisette.
❏ Gaming rooms from 1700. Restaurant 2000-2345. Galaxy 2300-0400
Tue.-Sun. ❏ Gaming rooms 80F. Galaxy 120F.
Casino as well as the Galaxy nightclub, overlooking the old harbour.

PALM BEACH CASINO Pl. Franklin Roosevelt (June-Oct.) and
Palais des Festivals et des Congrès (Nov.-May).
❏ 2000-0600. ❏ 60F.
Glamorous dinner-dance, cabaret and Le Jackpot disco. Smart dress.

CARLTON CASINO CLUB Hôtel Carlton Intercontinental,
58 Bd de la Croisette.
❏ 2200-0500. ❏ 60F.
Dine at La Belle Otero, dance in the piano bar or have a bit of a gamble!

CASINO LES FLEURS rue des Belges.
❏ Dinner-dance 2000-2330. Cabaret and shows from 2100. Gaming
rooms 1500-0300. ❏ 60F.
A casino with a sophisticated and colourful atmosphere.

LE JANE'S Hôtel Gray d'Albion, 38 rue des Serbes.
❏ Piano bar 2000-2230. Restaurant 2030-0300. Disco 2230-0600.
❏ Entry and first drink 100F. No entry fee if dining.
Piano bar and restaurant with fin de siècle décor, plus laser disco.

WHISKY À GOGO 115 Ave de Lérins.
❏ 2230-0530. ❏ Entry and first drink 120F.
Largest nightspot on the Riviera, complete with lasers and dry ice.

STUDIO CIRCUS 48 Bd de la République.
❏ 2230-0500. ❏ Entry and first drink 100F.
Top live cabaret and laser show frequented by film stars and tycoons.

RAGTIME 1 Bd de la Croisette.
❏ 2000-0200. ❏ Entry and first drink 80F. No entry fee if dining.
Restaurant and piano bar with New Orleans jazz most evenings.

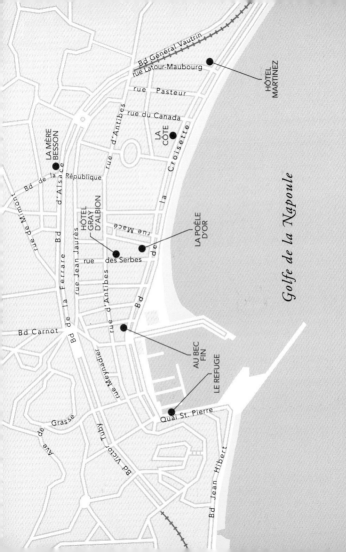

Restaurants

HÔTEL GRAY D'ALBION 38 rue des Serbes.
❑ 1200-1400, 2000-2230. Closed Feb. ❑ Expensive.
Four restaurants: Le Royal Gray is one of Cannes' best; Les 4 Saisons serves Provençal and Lebanese dishes; La Plage has a terrace on Bd de la Croisette; and finally, there's Le Jane's (see **CANNES-NIGHTLIFE**).

LA CÔTE Hôtel Carlton Intercontinental, 58 Bd de la Croisette.
❑ 1200-1400, 2000-2215 Thu.-Mon. ❑ Expensive.
Top-ranking cuisine. Try suprême de loup poêlé ratatouille *(sea bass and vegetable stew).*

LA MÈRE BESSON 12-13 rue des Frères-Pradignac.
❑ 1200-1430, 1945-2200 Mon.-Sat. Closed Feb. & lunch July & Aug.
❑ Expensive.
Good Provençal cuisine: bourride *and* pieds et paquettes *(pig's trotters).*

HÔTEL MARTINEZ 73 Bd de la Croisette.
❑ La Palme d'Or: 1200-1400, 2000-2200 Tue.-Sun. L'Orangerie: 1200-1415, 1945-2200. Both closed mid Nov.-mid Jan. ❑ La Palme d'Or: Expensive. L'Orangerie: Moderate.
La Palme d'Or has probably the best Provençal and modern cuisine in Cannes, served with Niçois Vin de Bellet. L'Orangerie is a larger, simpler restaurant with traditional dishes including roasted pig's trotters.

LA POÊLE D'OR 23 rue des États-Unis.
❑ 1200-1430, 2000-2215 Tue.-Sun. ❑ Moderate.
A discreet little restaurant known for its bourride, *roast duck, sauced waffles and a variety of fish dishes. Frequented by knowledgeable locals.*

AU BEC FIN 12 rue de 24 Août.
❑ 1200-1415 Mon.-Sat., 2000-2200 Mon.-Fri. ❑ Moderate.
Locals patronize this small bistro, with its reasonable prix-fixe menus.

LE REFUGE 13 Quai St. Pierre.
❑ 1200-1500, 2000-2200. Closed mid Nov.-mid Dec. ❑ Inexpensive.
Large bistro with good-value Provençal and freshly-caught fish dishes.

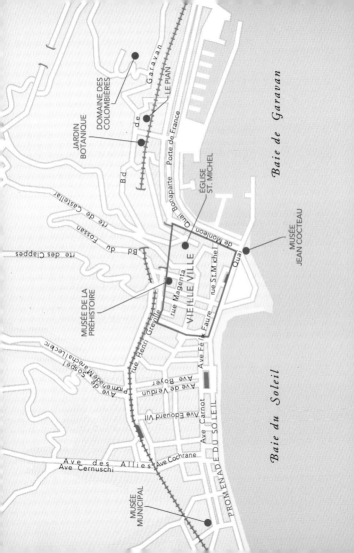

VIEILLE VILLE See MENTON-WALK.

ÉGLISE ST. MICHEL Parvis St. Michel.
A fine baroque church with green and yellow façade. The 15th-17thC campanile is 53 m high. Inside, note the altarpieces of St. Nicholas and St. Michel (1569), and the large 17thC organ. Chamber music concerts are held in the square in summer.

PROMENADE DU SOLEIL
Seaside esplanade with gardens, palm trees, hotels and restaurants facing a good shingle beach. At the west end is the village of Roquebrune, and to the east Musée Jean Cocteau and the Vieux Port.

MUSÉE JEAN COCTEAU Quai Napoléon III.
❏ 0900-1200, 1400-1800 Wed.-Sun. (Dec.-Oct.). ❏ Free.
Displays of Cocteau's (see A-Z) work in a 17thC fort. Note the paintings of Harlequin and the mosaic floor with its salamander design.

MUSÉE MUNICIPAL Palais Carnolès, 3 Ave de la Madone.
❏ 1000-1200, 1400-1800 Wed.-Mon. ❏ Free.
In the 18thC summer palace of the princes of Monaco, the museum houses a good beaux-arts collection. Modern paintings are on the ground floor (Sutherland, Poliakoff, etc.) and on the 1st floor are 13th-18thC European oil paintings, mainly French and Italian (Bréa, Maineri, Derain).

MUSÉE DE LA PRÉHISTOIRE rue Lorédan-Larchey.
❏ 1000-1200, 1400-1800 Wed.-Mon. ❏ Free.
This good prehistory and archaeological museum includes the skull of the famous Grimaldi Man (c.30,000 BC) plus local history displays and paintings by Dufy, Utrillo and Vlaminck.

LES COLOMBIÈRES Bd de Garavan.
❏ 0900-1200, 1500-2000 Wed.-Mon. (Jan.-Sep.). ❏ 15F.
A collection of three beautiful but separate gardens: Domaine des Colombières, Jardin Botanique and Le Pian.

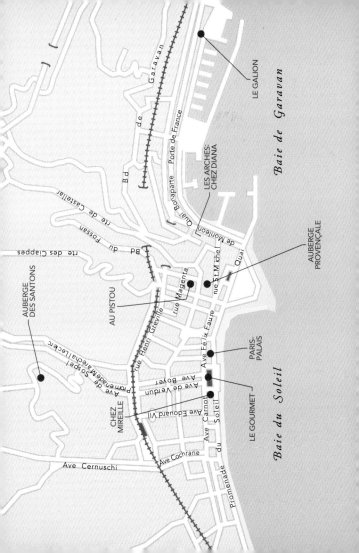

Baie de Garavan

LE GALION

LES ARCHES: CHEZ DIANA

AUBERGE PROVENÇALE

AU PISTOU

AUBERGE DES SANTONS

PARIS-PALAIS

CHEZ MIREILLE

LE GOURMET

Baie du Soleil

Bd   de   Garavan

Porte de France

Quai Bonaparte

Quai de Monleon

rte de Castellar

rte des Clappes

Bd du Fossan

rue St. Michel

rue Magenta

rue Henri Greville

Ave de Sospel

Promenade Maréchal Leclerc

Ave de Verdun

Ave Boyer

Ave Félix Faure

Ave Carnot

Ave Edouard VII

du Soleil

Promenade

Ave Cochrane

Ave Cernuschi

Restaurants

CHEZ MIREILLE Hôtel l'Hermitage, 1080 Promenade du Soleil.
❑ 1200-1430, 1945-2145 Wed.-Mon. Closed mid Nov.-mid Dec.
❑ Expensive.
Restaurant with a terrace, specializing in bouillabaise and fruits de mer.

LES ARCHES: CHEZ DIANA 31 Quai Bonaparte.
❑ 1200-1430, 2000-2300 Thu.-Tue. Closed Nov. ❑ Expensive.
Quayside bistro with good Provençal cuisine and English desserts.

AUBERGE DES SANTONS rte de l'Annonciade.
❑ 1200-1415 Tue.-Sun., 2000-2200 Tue.-Sat. Closed mid Nov.-mid
Dec. ❑ Moderate.
In a villa overlooking the sea near l'Annonciade monastery, the chef produces nouvelle cuisine, including mousseline des poissons (fish purée).

AUBERGE PROVENÇALE 11 rue Trenca.
❑ 1200-1415, 1945-2100 Tue.-Sun. ❑ Moderate.
Provençal and Norman cooking served in the hotel's rustic-style dining room. There are four good-value menus to choose from.

LE GOURMET Casino du Soleil, Promenade du Soleil.
❑ 1200-1430, 2000-2130 Wed.-Mon. Closed Nov. ❑ Moderate.
Top-class chef produces Provençal recipes nouvelle cuisine-style.

LE GALION Port de Garavan, 1 km northeast of Menton on the N 7.
❑ 1200-1415, 2000-2200 Wed.-Mon. Closed mid Oct.-Feb.
❑ Moderate.
Italian cuisine served in informal surroundings.

PARIS-PALAIS 1288 Promenade du Soleil.
❑ 1200-1415, 2000-2215. Closed mid Nov.-mid Dec. ❑ Moderate.
Smart restaurant with a terrace, palm trees and super views.

AU PISTOU 2 rue du Fossan.
❑ 1200-1415, 2000-2200 Wed.-Mon. Closed Nov. ❑ Moderate.
Good-value Provençal cooking including soups, fish dishes and shellfish.

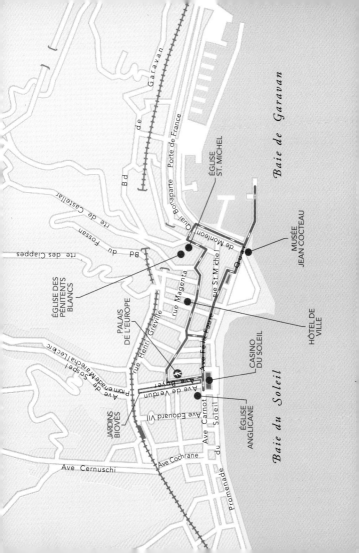

Walk

2 hr, excluding museum visits.

Start at the tourist office in Palais de l'Europe on the east side of the elegant Jardins Biovès. This park has flowers all year round, plus lemon and palm trees and statues, and is lined with restaurants and bistros. Turn left and walk 150 m to the Casino du Soleil. Just on the right in Ave Carnot is the Église Anglicane. However, turn left along Ave Félix Faure, parallel to Promenade du Soleil, left again into Pl. St. Roch and right on rue de la République. In the square lined with palm trees is the Italianate 17thC yellow and pink Hôtel de Ville. Inside is the civil marriage room decorated in 1957 with romantic scenes by the irrepressible Jean Cocteau (see **A-Z**). Keep walking gently uphill past the Église Reformée de France and Église des Pénitents Noirs along rue Général Gallieni and rue Longue. Now take a deep breath for the climb inland via Rampe St. Michel to Parvis St. Michel, a delightful small square which contains the Église St. Michel (see **MENTON-ATTRACTIONS**) and 17thC Église des Pénitents Blancs (with delicate façade). The view to the east is one of the best on the French Riviera, with the Vieux Port and Plage des Sablettes in the foreground, and in the background the three gardens (Les Colombières, Jardin Botanique and Le Pian) and the Italian Riviera. Up the hill are the Menton kasbah, the old Arab-style district, and the famous 19thC cemetery, reached by narrow twisting alleyways. But the route takes you down the tiered steps to Quai Bonaparte. Turn right to visit the 17thC bastion containing the Musée Jean Cocteau (see **MENTON-ATTRACTIONS**) on the corner of Quai Napoléon III. A stroll down the jetty gives views of the deep-blue Mediterranean and the yachts packed like sardines in the Port de Garavan. Walk west along Promenade du Soleil (see **MENTON-ATTRACTIONS**) and turn half-right into the little Pl. aux Herbes and rue Marins where you will find the main market (0530-1300), surrounded by little bistros. Past the market on the right is the pedestrianized rue St. Michel, lined with orange trees, boutiques and restaurants. Keep walking west along Ave Félix Faure in the direction of the Casino du Soleil. To the right, midway along rue Partouneaux, is the statue of Dr Bennett, who first extolled the beauty and climate of Menton in the 1850s.

In summer a tourist 'train' trundles along Promenade du Soleil to the harbour bastion (1000-1200, 1415-1900, 2030-2300).

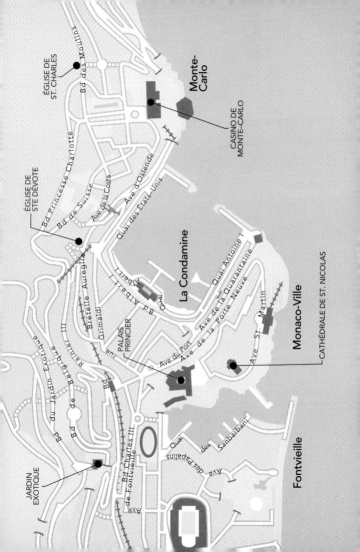

ÉGLISE DE
ST. CHARLES

Bd des Moulins

Monte-
Carlo

CASINO DE
MONTE-CARLO

ÉGLISE DE
STE DÉVOTE

Bd Princesse-Charlotte

Bd de Suisse

Ave de la Costa

Ave d'Ostende

Quai des États-Unis

La Condamine

Quai Antoine I

Ave de la Quarantaine

Ave de la Porte-Neuve

Bd du Jardin Exotique

Bd de Belgique III

Bd Rainier III

Breitelle Aureglia

rue Grimaldi

Quai Albert I

Bd Albert I

PALAIS
PRINCIER

Ave du Port

Ave St. Martin

Monaco-Ville

CATHÉDRALE DE ST. NICOLAS

JARDIN
EXOTIQUE

Bd de Fontvieille

Bd Charles III

Ave des Papalins

Quai des Sanbarbani

Fontvieille

PALAIS PRINCIER Pl. du Palais, Monaco-Ville.
❏ 0930-1830 June-Sep., 1000-1700 Oct. ❏ 30F.
*Built in the 13th-16thC in Italian Renaissance style, it overlooks the large cobblestoned square with its Louis XIV cannon and superb views. See the State apartments and Museé Napoléon (see **MONACO-MUSEUMS**). The main courtyard has three million white and coloured pebbles arranged in patterns. Note the 17thC Palatine chapel and Tour Ste Marie. The Compagnie des Carabiniers guard the palace, and change over at 1155.*

CATHÉDRALE DE ST. NICOLAS 4 rue Colonel Bellando de Castro, Monaco-Ville.
❏ 0800-1900, except during services.
In 19thC Romanesque/Byzantine style, it contains the tombs of former princes and princesses, including Grace, 'Gratia Patricia', behind the high altar. The episcopal throne is of Carrara marble and the reredos by Louis Bréa dates from 1500. Note the gilded statues of St. Bénoit and the Roman centurion in armour, St. Romanus. There is a sung Mass at 1000 Sun. (Sep.-June) by Les Petits Chanteurs de Monaco.

CASINO DE MONTE-CARLO Pl. du Casino.
*Built in 1878, it was designed by Charles Garnier, who was also responsible for the Paris opera house. The gardens, which have a dinosaur(!), are on top of a car park and conference centre. See **MONACO-NIGHTLIFE**.*

JARDIN EXOTIQUE Bd du Jardin Exotique.
❏ 0900-1900 May-Sep., 0900-1800 Oct.-April. ❏ 35F.
7000 varieties of subtropical flora. The prehistory observatory, with stalagmites and stalactites, is 60 m below. Allow 1.5 hr to visit both.

ÉGLISE DE STE DÉVOTE Pl. Ste Dévote, La Condamine.
❏ 0800-1200, 1400-1800.
12thC chapel, restored in 1870, in a canyon with precipitous cliffs.

ÉGLISE DE ST. CHARLES Ave St. Charles.
❏ 0800-1200, 1400-1800.
Built in 1883, it has 19 stained-glass windows and gilded chandeliers.

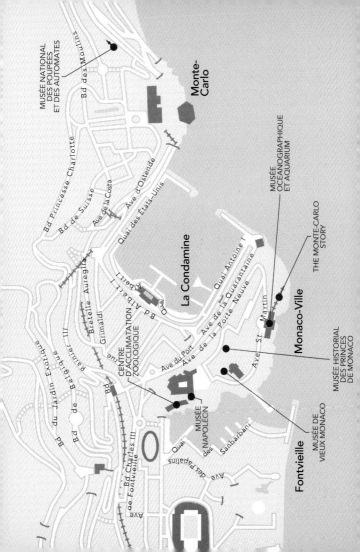

MUSÉE NATIONAL
DES POUPÉES
ET DES AUTOMATES

Bd des Moulins

Monte-
Carlo

Bd Princesse Charlotte

Bd de Suisse

Ave de la Costa

Ave d'Ostende

Quai des États-Unis

MUSÉE
OCEANOGRAPHIQUE
ET AQUARIUM

La Condamine

Quai Antoine I

Ave de la Quarantaine

THE MONTE-CARLO
STORY

Bretelle Aureglia

Rainier III

Grimaldi

Quai Albert I

Bd Albert I

Ave de la Porte Neuve

Monaco-Ville

CENTRE
D'ACCLIMATATION
ZOOLOGIQUE

Ave du Port

Ave St. Martin

MUSÉE HISTORIAL
DES PRINCES
DE MONACO

Bd du Jardin Exotique

Bd de Belgique

Bd Rainier III

Bd

Bd Charles III

Ave de Fontvieille

MUSÉE
NAPOLÉON

Fontvieille

Quai des Sanbarbani

MUSÉE DE
VIEUX MONACO

Ave des Papalins

Museums

MUSÉE NAPOLÉON Palais Princier, Pl. du Palais, Monaco-Ville.
❏ 1030-1230, 1400-1700 Tue.-Sun. (June-Nov.). ❏ 20F.
Housed in the south wing of the palace (see **MONACO-ATTRACTIONS**)*, the 1st floor is devoted to the history of the principality and the ground floor has a collection from the time of the First Empire. See* **Napoleon**.

MUSÉE OCEANOGRAPHIQUE ET AQUARIUM
Ave St. Martin, Monaco-Ville.
❏ 0900-2100 July & Aug., 0900-1900 April-June & Sep., 0930-1900 Oct.-Mar. ❏ 50F.
Built in 1910 by Prince Albert I, this massive building is 85 m high and includes 90 large fish tanks, a conference hall, laboratories and model ships. There are good views from the terrace. Allow 3 hr for a visit.

MUSÉE HISTORIAL DES PRINCES DE MONACO
27 rue Basse, Monaco-Ville.
❏ 0930-1900 Feb.-Oct., 1030-1700 Nov.-Jan. ❏ 20F.
Forty wax figures show key events from the Grimaldi (see **A-Z***) dynasty.*

MUSÉE DE VIEUX MONACO rue Émile de Loth, Monaco-Ville.
❏ 1430-1800 Mon., Wed. & Fri. (June-Sep.), 1400-1800 Wed. (Oct.-May). ❏ Free.
A small collection of costumes, pictures, books and pottery.

MUSÉE NATIONAL DES POUPÉES ET DES AUTOMATES
17 Ave Princesse Grace, Monte-Carlo.
❏ 1000-1830 Mar.-Sep., 1000-1215, 1430-1830 Oct.-Feb. ❏ 28F.
A collection of 400 dolls, automats, and sculptures in a terraced garden.

CENTRE D'ACCLIMATATION ZOOLOGIQUE Pl. du Canton.
❏ 0900-1200, 1400-1900. ❏ 25F.
A small zoo clinging to the cliff face overlooking the Port du Fontvieille.

THE MONTE-CARLO STORY Chemin des Pêcheurs.
❏ 1030-1730 Mar.-Nov., 1020-1130, 1430-1730 Dec.-Feb. ❏ 35F.
Audio-visual show on the history of Monaco and the Grimaldi (see **A-Z***).*

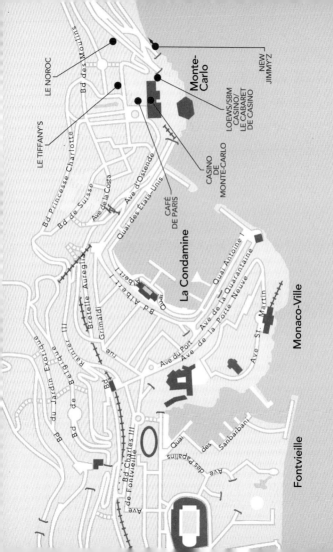

LE NOROC

Bd des Moulins

LE TIFFANY'S

Bd Princesse Charlotte

Bd de Suisse

Ave de la Costa

Ave d'Ostende

Quai des États-Unis

Bretelle Auréglia

rue Grimaldi

Bd Rainier III

Bd de Belgique

Bd du Jardin Exotique

Bd Charles III

Ave de Fontvieille

Monte-Carlo

NEW JIMMY'Z

LOEWS/SBM
CASINO/
LE CABARET
DE CASINO

CASINO DE
MONTE-CARLO

CAFÉ
DE PARIS

CASINO DE
MONTE-CARLO

La Condamine

Bd Albert I

Quai Albert I

Quai Antoine I

Ave de la Quarantaine

Ave de la Porte Neuve

Ave du Port

Ave St. Martin

Monaco-Ville

Quai des Papalins

Ave des Sanbarbani

Fontvieille

CASINO DE MONTE-CARLO Pl. du Casino.
❏ Slot machines from 1000. Salle Europe 1200-2400. Roulette and trente et quarante 1500-0200. Salons Touzet 1600-0200. ❏ Free entry to slot machines. Salle Europe 60F. Salons Touzet 100F.
The Orchestre National, and international opera and ballet companies perform in the Salle Garnier. Persons under 21 are not admitted to the gaming rooms and passports are required. See **MONACO-ATTRACTIONS**.

LOEWS/SBM CASINO 12 Ave des Spélugues.
❏ Gaming rooms 1700-0500. La Folie Russe: dinner-dance from 2030, cabaret at 2230 (Tue.-Sun.) ❏ Free entry to gaming rooms.
La Folie Russe is the sophisticated nightspot with a cabaret that has top-less dancers, nudes and vaudeville. Persons under 21 are not admitted.

LE CABARET DE CASINO In Loews/SBM Casino complex.
❏ Dinner-dance from 2100. Floor show at 2230 (Wed.-Mon., Sep.-June). ❏ Dinner-dance 400F. Floor show entry and first drink 150F.
Le London Express Orchestra plays for a formal, well-heeled clientele.

NEW JIMMY'Z Monte-Carlo Sporting Club, Ave Princesse Grace (July & Aug.) and Pl. du Casino (Sep.-June).
❏ 2300-0400. ❏ 220F.
Known as la plus belle discothèque. *Very smart, with lots of live shows.*

LE TIFFANY'S 3 Ave des Spélugues.
❏ 2300-0500 Wed.-Mon. ❏ Entry and first drink 150F.
The crowded parquet dance floor is surrounded by red armchairs and purple-painted walls; for the fashionable, more mature crowd.

LE NOROC 11 rue du Portier.
❏ 2200-0400. ❏ Entry and first drink 150F.
The glamorous 30+ crowd frequents this sophisticated piano bar/disco.

CAFÉ DE PARIS Pl. du Casino.
Now renovated, this smart café, brasserie, bar and newsagent with its terrace is still the best rendezvous in town. Start your evening here.

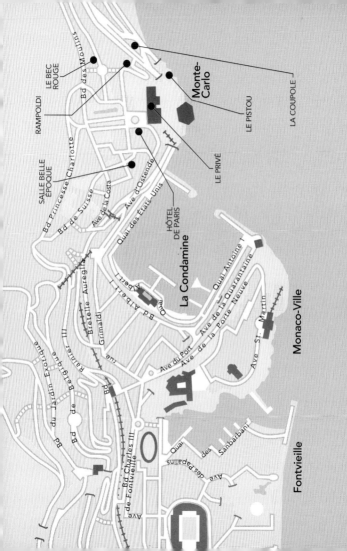

SALLE BELLE ÉPOQUE Hôtel Hermitage, Square Beaumarchais.
❏ 1200-1445, 2000-2245. ❏ Expensive.
*Classic cuisine in baroque surroundings. Try saumon cru aux courgettes
(salmon with courgettes) or lotte au gingembre et Sauternes (burbot in
ginger and Sauternes wine) served under frescoed ceilings.*

HÔTEL DE PARIS Pl. du Casino.
❏ Le Louis XV: 1200-1500, 2000-2300 Thu.-Mon. Le Grill de l'Hôtel
de Paris: 1200-1500, 2000-2300. Closed Dec. ❏ Expensive.
*Le Louis XV is on the ground floor, giving superb views of the square.
The cuisine is of an excellent quality. Ask for a table in the Empire
Room. The grillroom affords roof-top views of the Riviera. Try dorade
royale en filet cuite croustillante (fillet of sea bream with spices).*

LA COUPOLE Hôtel Mirabeau, 1 Ave Princesse Grace.
❏ 1200-1445, 2000-2245. Closed lunch July & Aug. ❏ Expensive.
*Impeccable service and cuisine, and a good wine cellar. Two menus are
on offer: Affaires and Gourmand.*

LE BEC ROUGE 11 Ave de Grande-Bretagne.
❏ 1230-1445, 2000-2230 Tue.-Sun. Closed Jan. ❏ Expensive.
*The candlelit tables are patronized by royalty. Try feuilleté aux morilles
(edible brown fungi) or navarin d'agneau (lamb stew). Best fish in town.*

LE PISTOU Hôtel Loews, 12 Ave des Spélugues.
❏ 1200-1430, 2000-2230. ❏ Expensive.
Monegasque cuisine served in a luxury hotel and casino complex.

LE PRIVÉ Casino de Monte-Carlo, Pl. du Casino.
❏ 1200-1445, 2000-2230 Wed.-Mon. ❏ Expensive.
French and Italian cuisine. Le Cabaret is in the same building.

RAMPOLDI 3 Ave des Spélugues.
❏ 1215-1430, 1930-2330. Closed Nov. ❏ Expensive.
*The smartest place in town. The specialities are soupe des poissons,
sole, sea bass and crêpe suzette.*

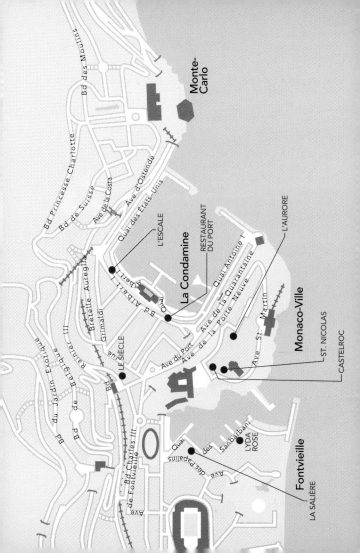

Monte-Carlo

Bd des Moulins

Bd Princesse Charlotte

Bd de Suisse

Ave de la Costa

Ave d'Ostende

Quai des États-Unis

L'ESCALE

RESTAURANT DU PORT

La Condamine

Quai Antoine I

L'AURORE

Ave de la Quarantaine

Ave de la Porte Neuve

Bd Albert I

Quai Albert I

Breteile Auréglia

Rue Grimaldi

Rue Princiere

Bd Rainier III

LE SIÈCLE

Bd de Belgique

Ave du Jardin Exotique

Bd Charles III

Ave de Fontvieille

Ave

Ave du Port

Ave St. Martin

Monaco-Ville

ST. NICOLAS

CASTELROC

Quai des

Ave des Papalins

Sanbarbani

LYDA ROSE

Fontvieille

LA SALIÈRE

Restaurants 2

LYDA ROSE 42 Quai des Sanbarbani, Fontvieille.
❑ 1200-1445 Mon.-Fri., 1745-2100 Mon.-Sat. ❑ Moderate.
Faces the palace and the marina. Try tournedos à la crème d'ail *(beef in cream and garlic) or* magret de canard à l'orange *(duck with orange).*

LA SALIÈRE Quai des Sanbarbani, Fontvieille.
❑ 1200-1430, 1800-2045 Mon.-Sat. Closed late Dec. ❑ Moderate.
Marina panoramas from the terrace. A good choice of fish dishes.

RESTAURANT DU PORT Quai Albert I, La Condamine.
❑ 1200-1430, 1800-2115 Tue.-Sun. Closed Nov. ❑ Moderate.
Italian cuisine, including fish dishes, risottos and ravioli di pesce alla maggiorana, *served on a terrace facing the port.*

L'ESCALE 17 Bd Albert I, La Condamine.
❑ 1145-1445, 2000-2200 Mon.-Sat. ❑ Moderate.
Modern restaurant with a terrace and harbour views. Try filet de loup *(sea bass) and* mêlé-mêlé de la mer *(seafood platter).*

LE SIÈCLE 10 Ave Prince Pierre.
❑ 1200-1430, 1800-2100. ❑ Moderate.
Speciality grills over a wood fire. Also try l'assiette de bouillabaisse.

CASTELROC Pl. du Palais, Monaco-Ville.
❑ 1130-1500 Sun.-Fri. Closed Dec. & Jan. ❑ Moderate.
Excellent views of the changing of the guard. Try truite saumoné aux amandes *(trout with almonds) and Monegasque stockfish.*

ST. NICOLAS 6 rue de l'Église, Monaco-Ville.
❑ 1200-1430, 2000-2200 Wed.-Mon. Closed Dec. & Jan.
❑ Inexpensive.
Try brochette de scampis grillés. *Good-value menus.*

L'AURORE 8 rue Princesse Marie de Lorraine, Monaco-Ville.
❑ 1130-1500, 2000-2130. Closed Dec. & Jan. ❑ Inexpensive.
Four modestly-priced menus. Try the dorade au feu *(smoked bream).*

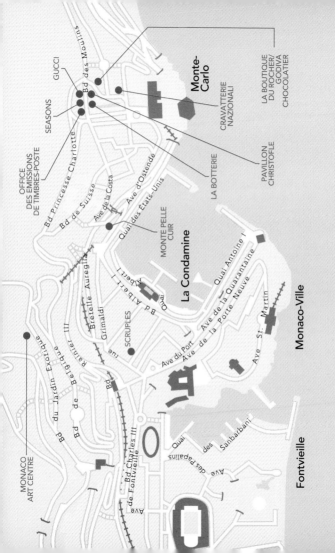

OFFICE
DES ÉMISSIONS
DE TIMBRES-POSTE

SEASONS

GUCCI

Bd des Moulins

Monte-
Carlo

CRAVATTERIE
NAZIONALI

LA BOTTERIE

PAVILLON
CHRISTOFLE

LA BOUTIQUE
DU ROCHER/
GODIVA
CHOCOLATIER

Bd Princesse Charlotte

Bd de Suisse

Ave de la Costa

Ave d'Ostende

Quai des États-Unis

MONTE PELLE
CUIR

La Condamine

Bretelle Aureglia

Quai Albert I

Bd Albert I

Quai Antoine I

Ave de la Quarantaine

Quai Antoine I

rue Grimaldi

SCRUPLES

Ave de la porte Neuve

Ave du Port

Ave St. Martin

Monaco-Ville

Bd de Belgique III

Bd du Jardin Exotique

Bd Rainier III

MONACO
ART CENTRE

Bd Charles III

Ave de Fontvieille

Quai des Sanbarbani

Ave des Papalins

Fontvieille

Shopping

See **Opening Times**.

MONACO ART CENTRE 45 Bd du Jardin Exotique.
Exquisite jewellery: jade, amethysts and coral worked in ceramic, glass, enamel, etc.

LA BOUTIQUE DU ROCHER 1 Ave de la Madone.
Quality Monegasque art and crafts products.

MONTE PELLE CUIR Park Palace, 27 Ave de la Costa.
Leather clothes and handbags of high quality.

GUCCI 39 Bd des Moulins.
Fine leather shoes, bags and accessories from the famous Italian firm.

LA BOTTERIE 14 Bd des Moulins.
Shoes by Bally, Charles Jourdan, Lariol, Kammer, etc.

SEASONS 31 Bd des Moulins.
Lingerie from Dior, Corrèges, Missoni, Céline, etc.

PAVILLON CHRISTOFLE 42 Bd des Moulins.
Fine porcelain from Limoges, Lalique, Baccarat, St. Louis, etc.

CRAVATTERIE NAZIONALI Galerie du Métropole.
Ten thousand ties and cravats from Dior, Givenchy, Dunhill and Missoni.

OFFICE DES EMISSIONS DE TIMBRES-POSTE
2 Ave St. Michel.
A philatelist's paradise; past and present stamps of Monaco.

SCRUPLES 9 rue Princesse Caroline.
A good selection of maps, guidebooks and literature in English.

GODIVA CHOCOLATIER 4 Ave de la Madone.
A fashionable salon de thé selling a wide range of chocolates.

Walks

Although the four segments of the principality are alternately at sea level (Fontvieille and La Condamine) and at hill-top level (Monaco-Ville and Monte-Carlo), thanks to a number of efficient, free lifts (ascenseurs), it is easy to scale the heights.

WALK 1: 1 hr. A 1.5 km stroll beside the sea, starting at Bd Albert I in La Condamine and continuing beside the port along Quai des États-Unis. Join Bd Louis II and walk beneath the Spélugues complex and Loews/SBM Casino (see **MONACO-NIGHTLIFE**) to the beach walk and gardens leading to Le Larvotto beach and Ave Princesse Grace. The walk ends at the Monte-Carlo Sporting Club.

WALK 2: 1 hr. A gentle walk starting at Pl. du Canton around the Port de Fontvieille admiring the motorized gin palaces and working yachts, the boutiques and smart seafood restaurants. At the seaward end of Quai des Sanbarbani turn right towards the pretty Jardin Rosier Princesse Grace, a 4 hectare site inaugurated in 1984 with 3500 rose trees of 150 sorts, plus streams and ponds. Guided tours are available of the nearby new athletics and sports complex which is home to the Monaco football team, one of the best in the French league. Ave du Prince Hereditaire Albert leads to the steps back to Pl. du Canton.

WALK 3: 2.5 hr. The most interesting walk is that round Monaco-Ville, on its rocky plateau reached by Rampe Major (there is also a lift at the east end). Palais Princier (see **MONACO-ATTRACTIONS**), with its museums (see **MONACO-MUSEUMS**) and colourful square, is at the western end; the huge Musée Oceanographique et Aquarium (see **MONACO-MUSEUMS**) is at the other. In between are the Cathédrale de St. Nicolas (see **MONACO-ATTRACTIONS**), Musée Historial des Princes de Monaco and Musée de Vieux Monaco (see **MONACO-MUSEUMS**), and the intriguing narrow streets of rue Basse, rue Comte Félix Gastaldi, the Italian Gothic law courts, Chapelle de la Paix and Pl. St. Nicolas, and the incomparable Jardins St. Martin facing the sea on the south side, with their fountains, statues, pergolas, Aleppo pines, aloes and tropical shrubs. You should also plan to see the changing of the royal guard, daily at 1155, in Pl. du Palais – a fascinating spectacle.

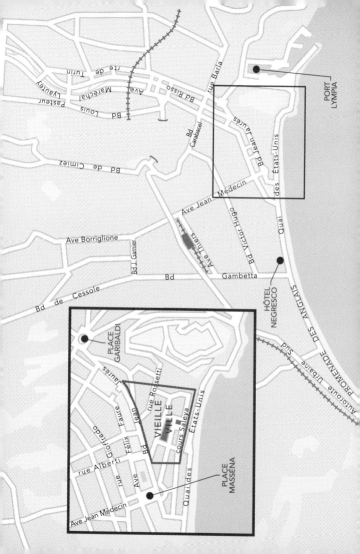

Attractions

PROMENADE DES ANGLAIS

This famous 4 km-long promenade was built in the 1820s and is lined with luxury hotels, boutiques and restaurants on one side, palm trees and gardens in the centre, and a shingle beach and the sea on the other. The airport is to the west, and the opera house and Le Château to the east. There are 15 beaches, most of which require a small fee to use.

VIEILLE VILLE In a triangle between the sea, Promenade du Paillon and Le Château.

The medieval souk-style quartier is north of the 17thC grid quartier with its fascinating blend of bistros, alleyways, little shops, the Cathédrale de Ste Réparate, l'Opéra de Nice, Hôtel de Ville and Palais de Justice.

PLACE MASSÉNA South end of Ave Jean Médecin.

A large square laid out between 1815 and 1835 with gardens and foun-tains in honour of Napoleon's (see A-Z) marshal. To the southwest are Casino Ruhl (see NICE-NIGHTLIFE), the beach and the Mediterranean.

PLACE GARIBALDI 300 m north of the Vieille Ville.

An Italian-style square with ochre-coloured buildings, a statue of Garibaldi (see A-Z), gardens and the Holy Sepulchre chapel. The Musée d'Histoire Naturelle (see NICE-MUSEUMS 2) is just to the northwest.

HÔTEL NEGRESCO 37 Promenade des Anglais.

One of the most famous hotels in the world, built in 1912 for six million gold francs. Classified as a monument historique, this large white 'wed-ding cake' edifice with its pink and blue dome, has a superb restaurant (Chantecler – see NICE-RESTAURANTS 1), the Salon Royale, chandeliers, works of art, Aubusson carpets and Edwardian-dressed doormen and bellboys.

PORT LYMPIA 200 m east of Le Château.

A rectangular harbour built in 1750 with the Bassin Lympia, Bassin des Amiraux and Bassin du Commerce containing a variety of yachts, fishing boats and ferries bound for Corsica. The port is surrounded by a mix of bars, taverns, bistros and marine suppliers.

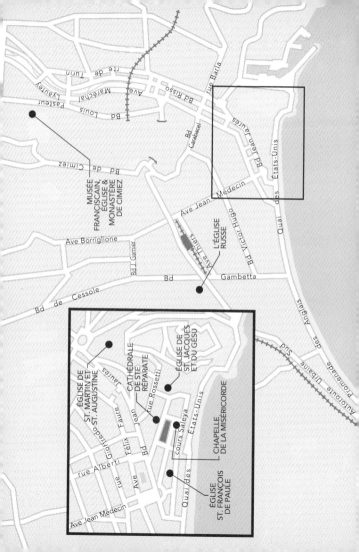

Churches

L'ÉGLISE RUSSE 17 Bd du Tzarewitch.
❑ 0900-1200 Mon.-Sat., 1430-1800 all week. ❑ Guided tours 15F.
This magnificent Russian Orthodox cathedral was built in 1903-12 in true 'Moscow' style, with six lovely green-gold onion domes. Note the superb icons and delicate frescoes.

CATHÉDRALE DE STE RÉPARATE Pl. Rossetti.
Built in 1650 in honour of the local saint, it has an 18thC bell tower with glazed tile dome, and a colourful baroque interior.

ÉGLISE DE ST. MARTIN ET ST. AUGUSTINE
Pl. St. Augustine.
Attractive baroque church where Martin Luther celebrated Mass in 1510 and where Garibaldi (see A-Z) was baptized. Note the Bréa altarpiece, and the Ségurane monument outside.

MUSÉE FRANCISCAIN, ÉGLISE & MONASTÈRE DE CIMIEZ Pl. du Monastère, Ave des Arènes de Cimiez.
The church of Nôtre-Dame de l'Assomption (1475-1515) has a notable Bréa pietà, crucifixion and deposition. The monastery dates from the 9thC, and there are also terraced gardens, 16thC cloisters and a Franciscan museum (1000-1200, 1500-1800; free).

ÉGLISE DE ST. JACQUES ET DU GÉSU rue Droite.
17thC baroque church with ornate chapels, 200 cherubim and a frescoed ceiling with scenes from St. James' life.

CHAPELLE DE LA MISÉRICORDE cours Saleya.
❑ Guided tours 1400-1800. ❑ Free, but donation expected.
An Italian baroque church built in 1740 by Guarini for the Black Penitents, with a Mirailhet altarpiece.

ÉGLISE ST. FRANÇOIS DE PAULE rue St. François de Paule.
❑ 0800-1200, 1400-1900.
Baroque church built in 1750 with a coloured-tile belfry, Van Loo painting and intricately grilled choir.

Excursion 1

A one-day excursion to Cagnes, St. Paul-de-Vence and Vence.

Drive west along Promenade des Anglais (N 98) parallel to the Autoroute du Sud and the sea, keeping Nice airport on your left, and cross the river Var on Pont Napoléon III. The Baie des Anges and a shingle beach are to the left. After you cross the little river Cagne and before you come to the large racecourse (Hippodrome), turn right on Bd J. F. Kennedy, cross Ave des Cannes to Bd Maréchal Juin and go beneath the autoroute, signposted Haut-de-Cagnes. Even if you get lost in Cagnes-Ville you will see the walled town on the hill 1 km north.

17 km – Haut-de-Cagnes (see **Cagnes-sur-Mer**). Park anywhere you can at the foot of the medieval town, and walk up montée de la Bourgade to explore the medieval town, the churches and the Chateau-Musée. If possible see Musée Renoir du Souvenir, 500 m east across the river Cagne. Take the D 36 due north for 7 km, then the D 2.

24 km – St. Paul-de-Vence (see **A-Z**). During a stroll around the village look out for the ramparts, inspect the art galleries and visit the incomparable Fondation Maeght on La Gardette hill. Continue for another 3 km on the D 2/Ave E. Hughes.

27 km – Vence (see **A-Z**). Park on the left at the main crossroads of Ave Foch and Pl. Maréchal Juin. The Matisse Chapelle du Rosaire is 400 m north on Ave H. Matisse, and the *vieille ville* is 500 m to the east. You now have a choice, depending on how much time is available.

Either: Travel west on the D 2210 via Tourrettes-sur-Loup, a charming fortified medieval village noted for its arts and craft centre, 15thC church and cultivated violets which are used in the production of perfume, Pont du Loup and Gorges du Loup (wolves were plentiful here in the days of the Grand Tour), for 25 km to Grasse (see **A-Z**). Continue south on the N 85 to Mougins (see **A-Z**) and join the autoroute (A 8) for a further 32 km back to Nice.

Or: From Vence take the D 2210 east to St. Jeannet, a pretty village among flower fields and orange groves, which produces a quality wine (see **A-Z**), and then Gattières, a hill-top village with vineyards and olive groves. From here a winding road leads to the river Var. Cross the bridge and join the major N 202 south for 11 km to link up with the N 7 or N 98 back into the western suburbs of Nice.

Excursion 2

A one-day excursion to Villefranche-sur-Mer, Beaulieu-sur-Mer and Èze.

Leave Nice past the port on the N 98, with the Musée Terra Amata on your left. The coast road, the Corniche Inférieure (see **Corniches**), has beautiful views (for passengers only!).

6 km – Villefranche-sur-Mer (see **A-Z**). There are two car parks near the tourist office. The Darse is the busy harbour and marina to the southwest, but the small port, *gare maritime* and lighthouse are set just below the old town. Out in the roadstead you will probably see a couple of sleek battle-grey frigates, perhaps an aircraft carrier and cruise liners, since this has been a beautiful natural deep-water harbour for 2000 years or more. There are two churches and two museums to visit, as well as a Vauban citadel and the *vieille ville*. Keep on the N 98, temporarily called Ave Albert, for 3.5 km, and as the road curves round just before Beaulieu-sur-Mer cross the railway on the D 25.

10 km – Cap-Ferrat. As this beautiful headland is only 2.5 km in length by 750 m across, you may like to park in the little port of St. Jean and spend an hour or so exploring on foot. There is an attractive cliff-top path which goes all the way round, taking in two beaches, gardens and the Fondation Ephrussi-de-Rothschild, an Italianate villa in seven hectares of elegant gardens which houses the Île de France museum (guided tours 1400-1900 Tue.-Sun., Dec.-Oct.; 30F). Also visit the zoo and tropical garden (0900-1900; 33F), semaphore station, lighthouse (*phare*), capes and bays, all of which ensure that this excursion will be memorable, if crowded in midsummer. Predictably, there are several top-class hotel-restaurants here, including Grand Hôtel du Cap-Ferrat, Royal Riviera and Voile d'Or. Rejoin the N 98 for 1 km.

11 km – Beaulieu-sur-Mer (see **A-Z**). Nicknamed Petite Afrique, the town, like Menton, claims to have the mildest Riviera winter. On the point overlooking the Baie des Fourmis is Villa Kerylos (1500-1900 Tue.-Sun., Dec.-Oct.; 18F), a handsome pseudo-Greek villa. There are a number of other elegant villas (Leonine and Namouna), the casino, a large marina and a pebbly beach. Follow the Corniche Inférieure round a number of headlands.

12 km – Èze (beach). The town (see **Èze**) has a split personality. At the foot of the 400 m-high outcrop is a resort, with its marina and beach.

On the top of the cliffs is one of the most picturesque hill villages on the Riviera. In order to reach it, there is a footpath for the energetic, but alternatively keep on the N 9 for 2 km to Cap d'Ail and take the steep winding road to the left up the hillside to join the Moyenne Corniche (N 7). Continue for 6 km.

20 km – Èze (village). Park in Pl. Général de Gaulle and walk up to see the medieval village with its narrow streets, artisans, boutiques and cafés. Visit the remains of the Ancien Château, the Jardin Exotique (all year; 10F) which surrounds it and from where there are astonishing panoramas (look for Corsica on the horizon), the church, chapel and the Fragonard scent factory (free). There are a number of interesting artisan shops (Anicroche, Benito, Aicardi) in the medieval village and beside the N 7. Restaurants include Château de la Chèvre d'Or, rue du Barri, with *huîtres chaudes au champagne* (oysters in champagne) and Nid d'Aigle, rue du Château. Return westwards on the Moyenne Corniche for 12 km, with the same attractive Mediterranean views as on the outward journey but seen from a couple of hundred metres higher up.

Of course you could do this same excursion comfortably by train from Nice; that is, if you are prepared to climb the hill to Èze village!

Èze

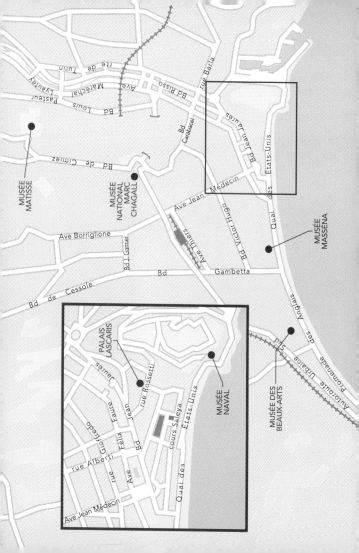

MUSÉE NATIONAL MARC CHAGALL rue Dr Ménard.
❏ 1000-1230, 1400-1730 Wed.-Mon. (Oct.-June), 1000-1900 (July-Sep.). ❏ 20F, under 18s free.
The main work is the 17 huge canvases, Message Biblique, *in rich entrancing colours. Also 39 gouaches, 205 sketches, 105 drawings and 215 lithographs, plus ceramics and rare books. See* **Chagall**.

MUSÉE MASSÉNA 65 rue de France/35 Promenade des Anglais.
❏ 1000-1200, 1400-1700 Tue.-Sun. (Dec.-Oct.). ❏ Free.
Regional history, religious art, costumes and 19thC Nice School paintings. See the Bonaparte, Murat and Masséna salons.

MUSÉE DES BEAUX-ARTS 33 Ave des Baumettes.
❏ 1000-1200, 1400-1700 Tue.-Sun. ❏ Free.
Princess Kotschoubey's 1876 mansion holds a vast 17th-19thC European art collection, including the Impressionists (Dégas, Boudin, Monet, Sisley) and collections of Chéret, Ziem, Van Dongen and Mossa.

MUSÉE MATISSE 164 Ave des Arènes de Cimiez.
❏ 1000-1200, 1400-1700 Tue.-Sun. Bus 15, 17, 20, 22. ❏ Free.
Renovated in 1991, this 17thC Genoese villa houses 180 paintings, 142 drawings and 60 bronze sculptures by the artist. The Matisse centre holds many temporary exhibitions – historic, thematic and contemporary – of interest to both adults and children. See **Matisse**.

PALAIS LASCARIS 15 rue Droite.
❏ 0930-1200, 1430-1800 Tue.-Sun. (Dec.-Oct.). ❏ Free.
This 17thC Genoese palace owned by the Lascaris-Vintimille family has baroque salons richly furnished with paintings, tapestries and gilt furniture. Note the 1738 pharmacy and grand staircase.

MUSÉE NAVAL Tour Bellanda, Le Château.
❏ 1000-1200, 1400-1900 Wed.-Mon. (mid Dec.-mid Nov.). ❏ Free.
This large 16thC round bastion clings to the rock face, has superb views and houses a collection of ship models, cannon, maps and paintings on the history of the port of Nice.

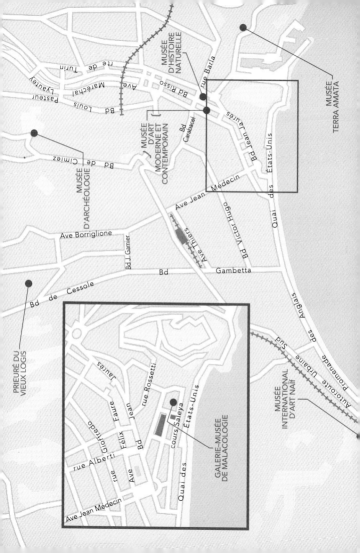

MUSÉE D'HISTOIRE NATURELLE (Barla) 60 bis Bd Risso.
❑ 0900-1200, 1400-1800 Wed.-Mon. (mid Sep.-mid Aug.). ❑ Free.
Concentrating on the history of evolution, palaeontology and mineralogy, the collection is housed in four main rooms. Also see the aquariums.

MUSÉE D'ARCHÉOLOGIE 164 Ave des Arènes de Cimiez.
❑ 1000-1200 Tue.-Sat., 1400-1800 Tue.-Sun. (Dec.-Oct.). Bus 15, 17, 20, 22. ❑ Museum free, Roman baths 8F.
A fine collection of Etruscan, Greek and Roman finds – jewellery, statues, ceramics, funeral lamps and vases. In 1989 the collection was renovated and moved to a site west of the 3rdC Roman baths.

MUSÉE TERRA AMATA 25 Bd Carnot.
❑ 0900-1200, 1400-1800 Tue.-Sun. ❑ Free.
Prehistory museum on a prehistoric site, with stone tools, bones and reconstructions of life around Nice 400,000 years ago.

GALERIE-MUSÉE DE MALACOLOGIE 3 cours Saleya.
❑ 1030-1300, 1400-1800 Tue.-Sat. (Dec.-Oct.). ❑ Free.
Large collection of seashells, fish, molluscs, etc.

MUSÉE INTERNATIONAL D'ART NAÏF Ave du Val-Marie.
❑ 1000-1200, 1400-1800 (May-Sep.), 1000-1200, 1400-1700 Wed.-Mon. (Oct.-April). ❑ Free.
6000 canvases by modern international artists.

MUSÉE D'ART MODERNE ET CONTEMPORAIN
Promenade du Paillon.
❑ 1100-1800 Wed. & Fri.-Mon., 1100-2200 Thu. ❑ Free.
Four large marble towers mark out this ultra-modern museum of international art of the last 70 years.

PRIEURÉ DU VIEUX LOGIS 59 Ave de St. Barthélemy.
❑ 1500-1700 Wed., Thu. & Sat., plus 1st Sun. in month. ❑ Free.
This reconstructed Dominican priory has displays on 16thC farm life, as well as a chapel, kitchen and study rooms.

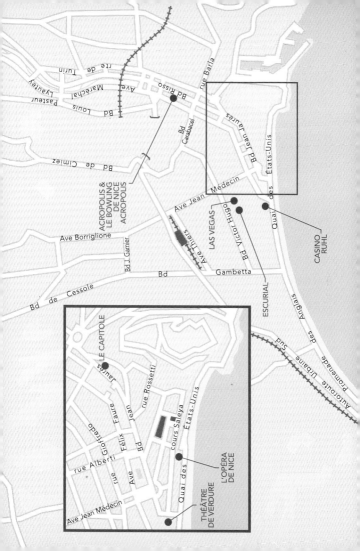

L'OPÉRA DE NICE 4 rue St. François de Paule.
A programme of opera, ballet, symphony concerts and chamber music throughout the year; home of the Nice Philharmonic Orchestra.

THÉÂTRE DE VERDURE Jardin Albert I, Promenade des Anglais.
Changing year-long programme of variety shows, jazz and ballet.

ACROPOLIS & LE BOWLING DE NICE ACROPOLIS
Palais des Arts, du Tourisme et des Congrès, Esplanade J. F. Kennedy/Ave Galliéni.
❑ Bowling 1100-0200. ❑ Bowling 30F.
Hosts every form of music, art, drama and dance, plus Holiday on Ice and international cat shows! Regular evening performances. Seats 2500. The bowling alley is the largest in France and also has billiards, snooker and a bar serving cocktails.

CASINO RUHL 1 Promenade des Anglais.
❑ Restaurant, cabaret and disco 2300-0400. Gaming rooms 1000-0500. ❑ Disco 170F. Free entry to gaming rooms.
Houses Le Louisiane restaurant, Le Grand Cabaret, the intimate Jok'Club discothèque, and opportunities for gambling, including roulette, trente et quarante, chemin de fer, punto banco and one-armed bandits.

ESCURIAL 29 rue Alphonse Karr.
❑ 2200-0400. ❑ Entry and first drink 80F.
Large disco with elaborate lighting effects. Lavish shows at weekends.

LE CAPITOLE 2 rue de la Tour, at the corner with Bd Jean Jaurès.
❑ Tea dance 1500-1900. Dinner-dance 2130-0200 Thu.-Sun. ❑ Tea dance, entry and first drink 50F. Dinner-dance 190F.
Dance to an excellent orchestra in sumptuous surroundings. Seats 700.

LAS VEGAS 8-10 rue du Maréchal Joffre.
❑ Brasserie 1100-2200. Disco 2100-0400. ❑ Entry and first drink 120F.
Decorated in American 'gambling' style, this is where the smart crowd dance the night away. Smart dress required.

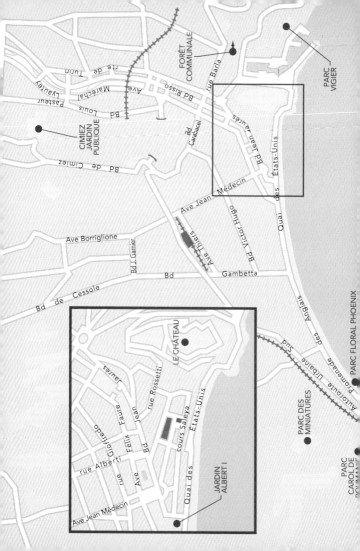

LE CHÂTEAU On a hill between the Vieille Ville and Port Lympia.
❏ 0900-2000 June-Aug., 0900-1900 Oct.-Mar. ❏ Free.
30 hectares of gardens with trees, shrubs, a waterfall, castle ruins, the Tour Bellanda (housing the Musée Naval – see NICE-MUSEUMS 1) and a restaurant. It can be reached by car, lift or tourist train, or on foot up rue des Pinchettes (400 steps).

JARDIN ALBERT I At the junction of Promenade des Anglais and Quai des États-Unis.
Plenty of benches for a rest in the shade of the palm trees near the Triton fountain and bandstand. The Théâtre de Verdure (see NICE-NIGHTLIFE) has open-air concerts in season. Start of the tourist train route.

PARC FLORAL PHOENIX 405 Promenade des Anglais.
❏ 1000-2100 Tue.-Sun. (Sep.-Dec. & Mar.-June). ❏ 70F.
A large complex with greenhouses, 'astronomic' gardens, a Maya temple, waterfalls, lakes, coffee shops and three restaurants.

CIMIEZ JARDIN PUBLIQUE 1.5 km north of the town.
Bus 15, 17, 20, 22. ❏ Free.
Having seen the two notable museums (Matisse and Archéologie – see NICE-MUSEUMS 1 & 2) and the Roman remains of the town of Cemenelum, this is an ideal place to rest and have a picnic. Jazz festival here in July.

PARC DES MINIATURES Bd Impératrice Eugénie.
PARC CAROL DE ROUMANIE Ave de Fabron.
Two open parks near the university, inland from Promenade des Anglais, with mini-golf, model villages and a new museum of 'nostalgia' (1000-1200, 1400-1900; 30F).

PARC VIGIER Bd Franck Pilatte.
Well laid out gardens opposite the gare maritime and overlooking the Club Nautique.

FORÊT COMMUNALE East of Port Lympia.
Large area of woodland and park between Mont Alban and Mont Boron.

Pl. du Palais, Nice

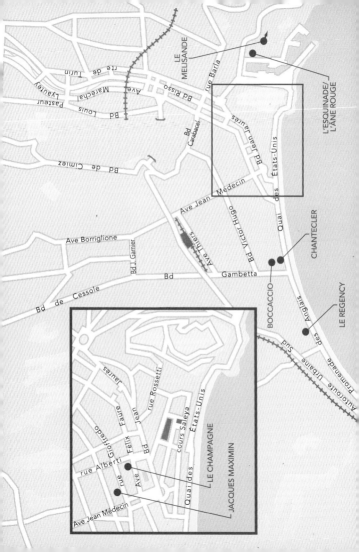

CHANTECLER Hôtel Negresco, 37 Promenade des Anglais.
❑ 1200-1500, 2000-2300. Closed mid Nov.-mid Dec. ❑ Expensive.
The best nouvelle cuisine *in the south of France, served in elegant surroundings. Try* loup à l'infusion de romarin *(sea bass with rosemary).*

L'ESQUINADE 5 Quai des Deux Emmanuel, Port Lympia.
❑ 1200-1430 Tue.-Sat., 2000-2215 Mon.-Sat. Closed Jan. ❑ Expensive.
Try the ratatouille or rouget à la crème de sauge *(mullet in sage sauce).*

L'ÂNE ROUGE 7 Quai des Deux Emmanuel, Port Lympia.
❑ 1200-1400, 2000-2145 Mon.-Fri. Closed mid July-late Aug.
❑ Expensive.
Regional dishes and seafood specialities, including bourride provençale.

LE CHAMPAGNE Grand Hôtel Aston, 12 Ave Félix Faure.
❑ 1200-1400 Mon.-Fri., 2000-2145 Mon.-Sat. ❑ Expensive.
Try foie d'oie aux poires confites au Sauternes *(goose liver in pears and Sauternes wine), served in style in a grand hotel.*

LE REGENCY Hôtel Beach Regency, 223 Promenade des Anglais.
❑ 1145-1415, 2015-2200 Mon.-Sat. ❑ Expensive.
The arlequin de saumon, mérou et courgettes crus à l'huile d'olive *(salmon, grouper fish and courgettes in olive oil) is recommended.*

BOCCACCIO 7 rue Masséna.
❑ 1200-1400, 2000-2300. ❑ Expensive.
Gastronomic Italian cuisine including spaghetti à la langouste.

LE MELISANDE Hôtel Palais Maeterlinck, 30 Bd M. Maeterlinck.
❑ 1200-1400 Tue.-Sun., 1945-2145 Tue.-Sat. Closed Jan. ❑ Expensive.
Nouvelle cuisine served in a chic hotel restaurant.

JACQUES MAXIMIN 2-4 rue Sacha Guitry.
❑ 1200-1500, 2000-2300 Tue.-Sun. ❑ Expensive.
Top-class cuisine served in the old Nice casino-theatre. Try loup en cocotte aux langoustines et champignons des bois.

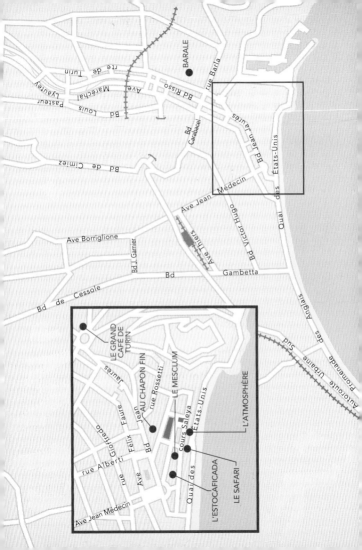

L'ATMOSPHÈRE 36 cours Saleya.
❑ 1200-1445, 2000-2215 Tue.-Sat. ❑ Expensive.
Try marmite des pêcheurs en bouillabaisse or sole soufflée aux lan-goustines at this excellent restaurant in the bustling flower market.

BARALE 39 rue Beaumont, tel: 93891794.
❑ 2000-2400 Tue.-Sat. Closed Aug. ❑ Moderate.
Eccentric family-owned restaurant established in 1870. The set menu is on the blackboard. Very popular with the locals; booking essential.

LE SAFARI 1 cours Saleya.
❑ 1145-1400 all week, 1945-2300 Tue.-Sun. ❑ Moderate.
Loud pop music and brusque service but good Niçois cuisine, including trouchia (omelette) and bagna cauda (hot garlic and anchovy sauce).

AU CHAPON FIN 1 rue du Moulin.
❑ 1145-1415 Tue.-Sat., 2000-2300 Mon.-Sat. Closed mid June-mid July. ❑ Moderate.
Many unusual dishes, including mille feuilles de magret de canard (duck in delicate layers of pastry) and paupiette de loup au coulis d'écrevisses (sea bass with crayfish sauce).

LE GRAND CAFÉ DE TURIN Pl. Garibaldi.
❑ 0800-2300. ❑ Moderate.
A large and popular but seedy pre-war Montparnasse-style café. Oysters are the speciality.

L'ESTOCAFICADA 2 rue de l'Hôtel de Ville.
❑ 1200-1400, 1930-2130 Sun.-Fri. Closed Nov. ❑ Inexpensive.
A small family-run bistro. Of course stockfish is on the menu, as well as bouillabaisse and squid.

LE MESCLUM 6 rue de la Terrasse.
❑ 1200-1415, 2000-2230. ❑ Inexpensive.
Waitresses in old Niçois dress serve traditional recipes including tian (gratin of rice) and mesclum (green salad).

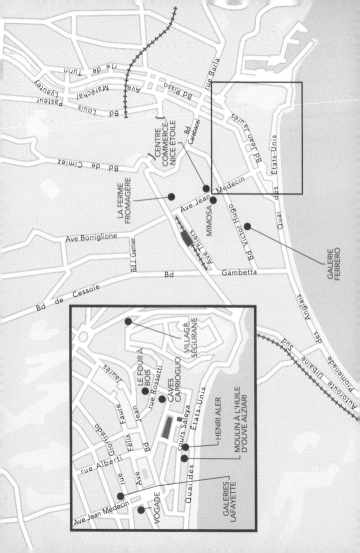

Shopping

See **Opening Times**.

GALERIES LAFAYETTE Pl. Masséna.
Major department store; a blend of Marks and Spencer and Woolworth.

CENTRE COMMERCE – NICE ÉTOILE 26 Ave Jean Médecin.
Large shopping mall with scores of individual shops.

GALERIE FERRERO 2-4 rue du Congrès.
Over 1000 posters, etc. of works by Chagall, Picasso, Braque and Miró.

HENRI ALER 7 rue St. François de Paule.
Wide selection of home-made crystallized fruits, chocolates and pastries.

MOULIN À L'HUILE D'OLIVE ALZIARI
14 rue St. François de Paule.
Small shop selling own produce; olives, olive oil, honey and rose-water.

VOGADE 1 Pl. Masséna.
Pastries, patisserie and cakes of incomparable lightness and flavour.

LA FERME FROMAGÈRE 13 rue Assalit.
A wonderful array of the best cheeses from the south of France.

MIMOSA 27 Ave Jean Médecin.
Local confections: calissons, chardons, grimaldines *and* perlines.

LE FOUR À BOIS 37 rue Droite.
The biggest choice of bread in Nice. There are 16 different sorts, including garlic, aniseed, thyme and caraway seed.

CAVES CAPRIOGLIO 16 rue de la Préfecture.
Superb range of wines, including the local Bellet, Bandol and St. Tropez.

VILLAGE SÉGURANE 28 rue Catherine Ségurane.
A large and varied antiques market with individual stalls.

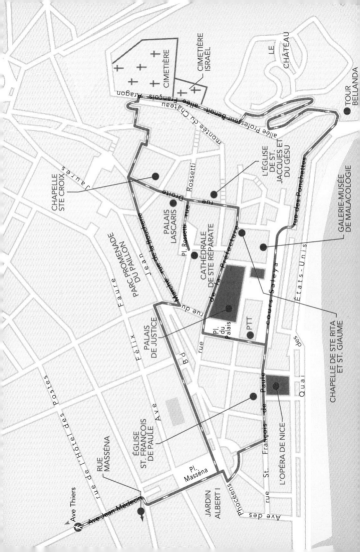

CIMETIÈRE

CIMETIÈRE ISRAËL

LE CHÂTEAU

TOUR BELLANDA

allée Professeur Benoit — François Aragon

montée du Château

CHAPELLE STE CROIX

L'ÉGLISE DE ST. JACQUES ET DU GÉSU

Jaures

Rue Rossetti

Rue Droite

GALERIE-MUSÉE DE MALACOLOGIE

Rue des Ponchettes

PALAIS LASCARIS

Pl. Rossetti

CATHÉDRALE de STE RÉPARATE

Rue de la Boucherie

Jean

Faure

PARC PROMENADE DU PAILLON

Rue du

États-Unis

Cours Saleya

CHAPELLE DE STE RITA ET ST. GIAUME

Félix

PALAIS DE JUSTICE

Bd

Pl. du Palais

PTT

Rue

Quai des

postes

Ave

rue de l'Hôtel des postes

ÉGLISE ST. FRANÇOIS DE PAULE

Ave

rue St. François de Paule

L'OPÉRA DE NICE

RUE MASSÉNA

Pl. Masséna

JARDIN ALBERT I

Phocéens

rue St.

Ave des

Ave Thiers

Ave Jean-Médecin

Walk

2 hr.

Start at the tourist office next to the SNCF in Ave Thiers. Turn left and after 100 m turn right on the long bustling Ave Jean Médecin, which runs for nearly 1 km to Pl. Masséna (see **NICE-ATTRACTIONS**). This is the main, but not the smartest, shopping street. After 250 m on the right is the Basilique Nôtre-Dame de l'Assomption (0730-1200, 1430-1900). A further 500 m on, also on the right, is rue Masséna, pedestrianized and leading to the post office, Anglican church, another tourist office, Musée Masséna (see **NICE-MUSEUMS 1**) and Hôtel Negresco (see **NICE-ATTRACTIONS**), but keep on into the large Pl. Masséna (see **NICE-ATTRACTIONS**) with its gardens, fountains and benches. To the left is the Parc Promenade du Paillon, leading up to the *gare routière* (bus station) and the huge modern Acropolis (see **NICE-NIGHTLIFE**). To the right are the Jardin Albert I (see **NICE-PARKS & GARDENS**), Théâtre de Verdure (see **NICE-NIGHTLIFE**), Casino Ruhl (see **NICE-NIGHTLIFE**) and Promenade des Anglais (see **NICE-ATTRACTIONS**). Walk across the square into rue de l'Opéra and turn left into rue St. François de Paule. On the left is the baroque church of the same name (see **NICE-CHURCHES**) and on the right L'Opéra de Nice (see **NICE-NIGHTLIFE**). Watch out for gypsies, who can be very persistent in their demand for money. Tempting local shops include Henri Aler and Moulin à l'Huile d'Olive Alziari (see **NICE-SHOPPING**), and several bistros, including Romain and L'Atmosphère (see **NICE-RESTAURANTS 2**). At the end is cours Saleya, with a colourful flower market surrounded by a dozen dazzling little restaurants. Just beyond is the artisan/antiques market. Turn left into rue Louis Gassin past the post office and continue to Pl. du Palais. On the right is the colossal Palais de Justice and campanile clock tower. Turn right into rue de la Préfecture and on the right are the 18thC government palace, Caves Caprioglio (see **NICE-SHOPPING**) and the baroque Chapelle de Ste Rita et St. Giaume, which has a noteworthy marble altarpiece. Turn left on rue Droite, a narrow street with bistros and bakeries, and patisseries which make *tourte de blé* and meringues. La Taverne du Château serves *tripes niçoise*. L'Église de St. Jacques et du Gésu (see **NICE-CHURCHES**), built in 1607, is on the right. Keep on for 50 m and make a detour left for 100 m down rue Rossetti to the Cathédrale de Ste Réparate (see **NICE-CHURCHES**). This splendid mid-17thC baroque church honours the

patron saint of Nice who was martyred in Asia, and is set in a handsome little square. Look inside for the statue of Joan of Arc in shining armour, and holding a flag, with her skirt decorated with fleur-de-lys. Retrace your footsteps to rue Droite, turn left past Scarlett's nightclub and several art galleries, and on the left is the yellow façade of the 17thC Palais Lascaris (see **NICE-MUSEUMS 1**).

You now have a choice of routes.

Either: Turn left on rue du Collet to Pl. Centrale, rue de la Boucherie and rue du Marché into the main Bd Jean Jaurès and Parc Promenade du Paillon, a 1 km-long strip of public gardens, complete with palm trees, fountains and benches, which follows the line of the underground river Paillon. On reaching Pl. Masséna you can retrace your route back to Ave Thiers.

Or: Turn right into rue Ste Claire and climb steadily past the yellow Chapelle Ste Croix with its clock tower, the convent of Les Pénitents Blancs and hospice of the Petites Soeurs des Malades, and climb the steps to the top of the hill. On your left is a huge cemetery, but turn right past the smaller Israel cemetery and follow wide gentle paths up to the summit of Le Château (see **NICE-PARKS & GARDENS**), with a waterfall, castle ruins and a *table d'orientation*, from where there are truly superb views of Nice and the Mediterranean. There is also a modest bistro which caters for weary travellers! The way down is to the south, either via the lift (0900-2000 June-Aug.), or by steps to the Tour Bellanda, which now houses the Musée Naval (see **NICE-MUSEUMS 1**), and is where Berlioz, the 19thC Romantic composer, lived. At the foot of the steep cliffs is Pl. du 8 Mai 1945. Turn right and follow rue des Ponchettes. The Galerie-Musée de Malacologie (see **NICE-MUSEUMS 2**) is at the end in cours Saleya. From here you can retrace your footsteps to Pl. Masséna, Ave Jean Médecin and Ave Thiers.

In summer a tourist 'train' operates between Casino Ruhl, the flower market, the *vieille ville* and Le Château.

Le Château, Nice

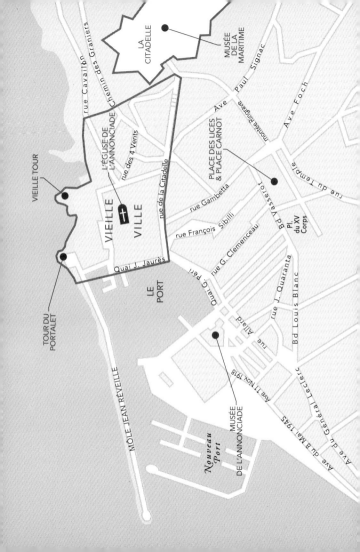

LA CITADELLE

MUSÉE DE LA MARITIME

rue Cavaillon

rue des Graniers

Chemin des Graniers

rue des 4 Vents

Ave. Paul Signac

montée Ringrave

Ave Foch

L'ÉGLISE DE L'ANNONCIADE

VIEILLE TOUR

VIEILLE VILLE

rue de la Citadelle

PLACE DES LICES & PLACE CARNOT

rue du Temple

rue Gambetta

rue François Sibilli

Bd Vasserot

Pl. du XV Corps

rue G. Clemenceau

rue J. Quaranta

TOUR DU PORTALET

Quai J. Jaurès

LE PORT

Quai G. Péri

rue Allard

Bd Louis Blanc

MÔLE JEAN RÉVEILLE

Ave 11 Nov 1918

Ave du 8 Mai 1945

Ave du Général Leclerc

Nouveau Port

MUSÉE DE L'ANNONCIADE

LE PORT & MÔLE JEAN RÉVEILLE

In summer scores of smart yachts with nubile crews, vie for space with ferries and fishing boats, surrounded by cafés, boutiques, galleries and Provençal-coloured houses. Café Senequier, with its large terrace overlooking the port, or Le Girelier (see **ST. TROPEZ-RESTAURANTS***) provide a colourful panorama of the teeming crowds. A walk along the 500 m northern mole from Tour du Portalet gives excellent views. The western Nouveau Port is for smaller yachts. Boat trips, tel: 94965100, leave from Quai de l'Épi and Môle Jean Réveille in summer for Port-Grimaud, Ste Maxime, St. Raphaël and the Îles de Lérins (see* **Islands***).*

VIEILLE VILLE Between La Citadelle and Le Port.

In the narrow streets look out for Château de Suffren, Église de l'Annonciade, the Vieille Tour and Hôtel de Ville.

PLACE DES LICES & PLACE CARNOT

In the centre of town, these two squares have Tue. and Sat. markets, and boules competitions. Sip an apéritif at Café des Arts (see **ST. TROPEZ-RESTAURANTS***) and spot the film stars and magnates among the local pétanque-players. Nearby rue François Sibilli is the place to shop.*

MUSÉE DE L'ANNONCIADE rue de la Nouvelle Poste.

❏ 1000-1200, 1400-1800 Wed.-Mon. (Dec.-Oct.). ❏ 25F.
Converted chapel housing works by Signac, Dufy, Matisse, Bonnard and Utrillo from period when painters 'discovered' St. Tropez (1890-1930).

LA CITADELLE rue de la Citadelle.

❏ 1000-1830 Wed.-Mon. (mid June-mid Sep.), 1000-1700 (mid Sep.-mid Nov. & mid Dec.-mid June). ❏ Free.
A powerful hexagonal 17thC fortress on a hill, with a keep, three round towers, fortified ramparts and fine views of St. Tropez, Ste Maxime, Port-Grimaud and the Maures Massif mountains.

MUSÉE DE LA MARITIME In La Citadelle keep.

❏ 1000-1200, 1500-1900 Fri.-Wed. (Jan.-Oct.). ❏ 15F.
Ship models, cannon, torpedoes and World War II 'reminders'.

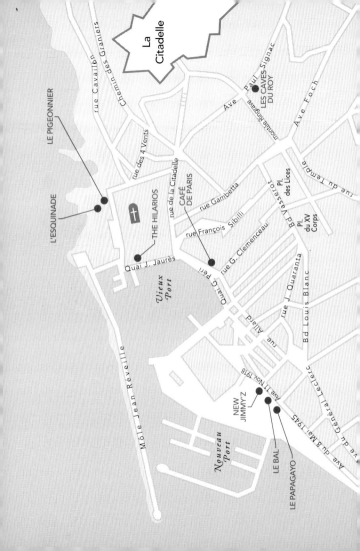

La Citadelle

rue Cavaillon

Chemin des Graniers

rue des 4 Vents

Paul Signac

LES CAVES DU ROY

Ave Paul

montée anglaise

Ave Foch

rue de la Citadelle

CAFÉ DE PARIS

rue Gambetta

rue du Temple

LE PIGEONNIER

L'ESQUINADE

THE HILARIOS

Quai J. Jaurès

rue François Sibilli

rue G. Clemenceau

Bd Vasserot

Pl. des Lices

Pl. du XV Corps

Quai Péri

Vieux Port

Môle Jean Réveille

rue J. Quaranta

Bd Louis Blanc

rue Allard

NEW JIMMY'Z

Ave 11 Nov. 1918

Nouveau Port

LE BAL

LE PAPAGAYO

Ave du 8 Mai 1945

rue du Général Leclerc

Nightlife

LES CAVES DU ROY Hôtel Byblos, Ave Paul Signac.
❏ 2230-0500 mid June-mid Sep. ❏ Entry and first drink 140F.
The Riviera's most fashionable disco and the best live entertainment in town. Jacqueline Vaissière introduces the showbiz stars. Smart dress.

NEW JIMMY'Z Résidence du Nouveau Port.
❏ 2300-0600. ❏ Entry and first drink 100F.
Up-and-coming smart nightclub run by Régine, in competition with Les Caves du Roy.

LE PAPAGAYO Résidence du Nouveau Port.
❏ 2300-0600 June-Sep. ❏ Entry and first drink 90F.
A popular nightspot with une folle *ambience. Phillipe Corti is your MC.*

LE PIGEONNIER 11-13 rue de la Ponche.
❏ 2300-0500 June-Sep. ❏ Entry and first drink 80F.
The top gay disco and meeting place in town, with great music.

LE BAL Résidence du Nouveau Port.
❏ 2300-0700 May-Oct. ❏ Entry and first drink 90F.
A white-tiled gay disco situated above the boutiques. Enjoy live music from Sophie and her band.

L'ESQUINADE rue du Four.
❏ 2300-0400. ❏ Entry and first drink 90F.
A traditional and noisy disco-nightclub.

THE HILARIOS Quai Jean Jaurès.
❏ 1630-0600. ❏ Before 2230 50F, after 2230 80F.
A piano bar decorated in a maritime vein, with music by Amar and Phillippe. Live jazz bands perform twice a week in season, and there is a disco until dawn on the other five days.

CAFÉ DE PARIS Hôtel Sube, 15 Quai Suffren.
❏ 0800-0300 May-Oct., 0800-1900 Nov.-April.
Zinc bar with a fin de siècle *atmosphere; popular with yachting crowd.*

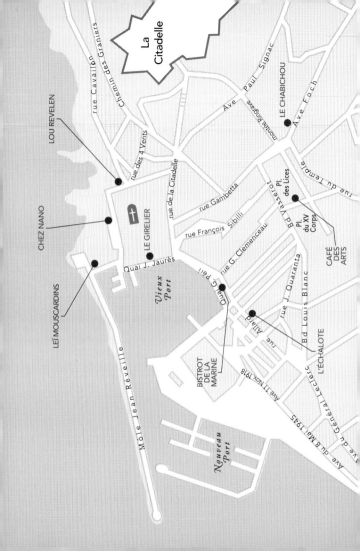

La Citadelle

rue Cavaillon

Chemin des Graniers

Ave. Paul Signac

montée Ringrave

LE CHABICHOU

Ave Foch

LOU REVELEN

rue des 4 Vents

rue de la Citadelle

rue Gambetta

Pl. Vasserot

Pl. du XV Corps

Bd Vasserot

rue du Temple

CHEZ NANO

rue François Sibilli

rue G. Clemenceau

CAFÉ DES ARTS

LEÏ MOUSCARDINS

LE GIRELIER

Quai J. Jaurès

Vieux Port

Quai G. Péri

rue J. Quaranta

Bd Louis Blanc

rue Allard

L'ÉCHALOTE

Môle Jean Réveille

BISTROT DE LA MARINE

Ave 11 Nov 1918

Ave du Général Leclerc

Ave du 8 Mai 1945

Nouveau Port

Restaurants

LE CHABICHOU Ave Foch.
❑ 1230-1500, 2000-2300. Closed Nov.-mid Dec. ❑ Expensive.
Try daube aux pieds de porc et févettes *(pig's trotter and bean casserole)*
or soufflé aux saveurs exotiques. *The best* nouvelle cuisine *on the coast.*

CHEZ NANO Pl. de l'Hôtel de Ville.
❑ 1200-1500, 2000-2400. Closed Jan.-Mar. ❑ Expensive.
An ultra-smart, noisy restaurant in which to see and be seen.

LE GIRELIER Quai Jean Jaurès.
❑ 1230-1430, 2030-2300. Closed Jan.-Mar. ❑ Expensive.
The specialities here are shellfish, bourride, bouillabaisse *and local*
white wines.

LEÏ MOUSCARDINS Quai Frédéric Mistral.
❑ 1215-1500, 2015-2315. Closed Nov.-Jan. ❑ Expensive.
Some of the best cuisine in St. Tropez, as well as a wide range of local
wines and good sea views.

CAFÉ DES ARTS Pl. des Lices.
❑ 1200-2330. Closed Oct.-Mar. ❑ Moderate.
A popular but shabby café with unassuming cuisine.

BISTROT DE LA MARINE Quai Gabriel Péri.
❑ 1215-1500, 2015-2300. ❑ Moderate.
A good-value, medium-priced restaurant alongside the port. The hors
d'oeuvre and fish dishes are recommended.

L'ÉCHALOTE 35 rue Allard.
❑ 1215-1415, 2015-2230. Closed mid Nov.-mid Dec. ❑ Moderate.
The grubby exterior hides a restaurant with a terrace overlooking the
port, which serves excellent fish cuisine.

LOU REVELEN 4 rue des Remparts.
❑ 1200-1430, 2015-2300. Closed Nov.-Jan. ❑ Moderate.
Regional and Italian dishes. Try the stuffed sardines and salade niçoise.

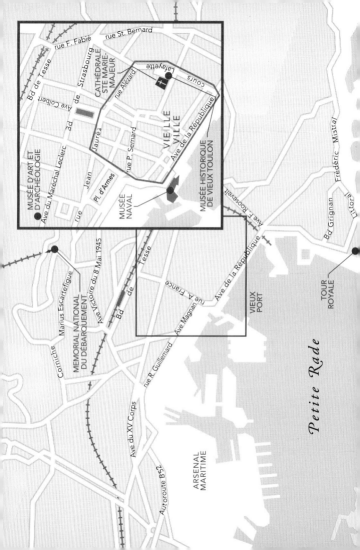

VIEILLE VILLE Inland from Quai Stalingrad.
*Fortunately undamaged during World War II (see **A-Z**), the old town is mainly pedestrianized and has alleyways, cafés, boutiques and tiny paved squares with palm trees, flowers and markets. Visit Pl. Puget, rue d'Alger, cours Lafayette (morning market), Cathédrale Ste Marie-Majeur, theatre, fish market and Les Halles (covered market).*

CATHÉDRALE STE MARIE-MAJEUR Traverse Cathédrale.
❏ 0800-1200, 1400-1900.
A mix of styles, ranging from 11th-12thC Romanesque to Gothic to a bell tower of 1740. The gloomy interior has many works by the 17thC Puget family.

MUSÉE HISTORIQUE DE VIEUX TOULON cours Lafayette.
❏ 1400-1800 Mon.-Sat. ❏ 10F.
*History of the town and region, and Napoleon (see **A-Z**) memorabilia.*

MUSÉE D'ART ET D'ARCHÉOLOGIE Ave du Maréchal Leclerc.
❏ 1000-1200, 1500-1800 Tue., Wed. & Fri.-Sun. ❏ 20F.
*Ground floor has natural history, Gallo-Roman remains, and Greek and Egyptian finds. The 1st floor has a collection of Provençal and Riviera artists including Fragonard (see **A-Z**), Vernet, Van Loo and Vlaminck.*

MUSÉE NAVAL Pl. d'Ingénieur Général Monsenergue.
❏ 1000-1200, 1330-1800 Tue.-Sun. Closed Tue. out of season. ❏ 20F.
Interesting collection with models of 18thC ships, paintings, statues, drawings and vintage submarines. The 16thC Tour Royale (1000-1800 April-Oct.; 15F), 2 km south on Pointe de la Mitre, once a prison, is now an annexe to the museum.

VIEUX PORT (DARSE VIEILLE)
*From Quai Stalingrad, rebuilt in 1945, there are views of the French navy, arsenal and huge roadsteads. Boat trips can be made to St. Mandrier-sur-Mer (headland with a fort and prison) or to the Îles d'Hyères (see **Islands**), and there is a day-long cruise to St. Tropez. A French warship is usually on view on summer weekends.*

Attractions 2

ARSENAL MARITIME
❑ Guided tours from Quai Stalingrad 0900-1100, 1400-1630.
❑ Free, but donation expected.
240 hectares of 17thC repair quays, graving docks and dry docks.

MEMORIAL NATIONAL DU DÉBARQUEMENT
Tour Beaumont, rue Edouard Perrichi, 3 km north of Toulon.
❑ Cable car 0915-1200, 1415-1800 Tue.-Sun. Museum and zoo 0930-1130, 1430-1815. ❑ Cable car 25F return. Museum 25F. Zoo 30F.
A cable car will take you to the top of Mont Faron. In the tower are the Allied war memorial and a small museum with displays and films on the 1944 landings (see **World War II***). You should also see the nearby zoo and enjoy the beautiful views over the city and the roadstead.*

Sanary-sur-Mer

Excursions

EXCURSION 1: *Half day to Bandol, including an optional boat trip.*

From the town centre take Quai Stalingrad and follow the D 559 coast road (not the A 50) and the D 18.

6 km – Fort Balaguier. An industrial town with shipyards, a marina and fishing boats. The fortress, captured from English marines in 1793 by Napoleon (see **A-Z**) now houses a naval museum (1000-1200, 1400-1800 Wed.-Sun.; 10F), and has gardens and views of the roadstead. After Tamaris and Les Sablettes take the D 16 for 4 km to Six-Fours-les-Plages. To the south are beaches, forests, the pilgrimage chapel of Nôtre-Dame du Mai on Cap Sicié, and Île des Embiez (reached by ferry from Port de Brusc; 15F return) (see **Islands**). Keep on the D 559 north-west via Sanary-sur-Mer, a fishing port with a beach, and Le Brusc.

20 km – Bandol (see **A-Z**). Past the casino on the left are the marina and port. From Bandol it is 17 km on the A 50 back into Toulon.

EXCURSION 2: *Half day to Hyères, including an optional boat trip.*

Leave Toulon along Quai Stalingrad and Rond-Point du Général Bonaparte, then follow the D 42 coast road past Cap Brun and Point Ste Marguerite to join the D 559. Two kilometres after Le Pradet take the D 76/D 276 into the southern suburbs of Hyères.

22 km – Hyères (see **A-Z**). After looking at the medieval hill town, call in at the Jardins Olbius Riquier in the southeastern suburbs. Find Ave St. Hilaire, which joins the D 559. Now follow the roads southwest of Toulon/Hyères airport to Hyères-Plage. From Port d'Hyères ferries sail to the three Îles d'Hyères (see **Islands**). The tourist office in Hyères will give you ferry times and prices as they vary during the year. Continue south along the eastern isthmus on rte de la Capte.

33 km – Presqu'Île de Giens. On the south side at the little port of La Tour Fondue is another short ferry crossing to the Îles d'Hyères. Bd E. Herriot continues west to the resort village of Giens, where the poet St.-John Perse used to live. The Hôtel-Restaurant Provençal has a fine reputation, and also has a private beach. Return to the mainland via the western sand spit, rte de Sel, through salty marshland, and turn left at L'Almanarre on the D 559 for 19 km along the coast to Toulon.

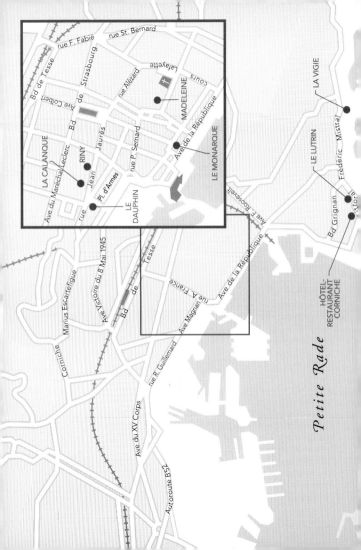

Restaurants

LE LUTRIN 8 Littoral Frédéric Mistral.
❏ 1200-1400, 1900-2100 Sun.-Fri. Closed June. ❏ Expensive.
Toulon's smartest restaurant, situated in a 19thC villa. Try beouf à la ficelle grand-mère (grandma's beef stew with tomato sauce).

LA VIGIE 57 Littoral Frédéric Mistral.
❏ 1200-1400 Thu.-Tue., 1915-2115 Mon., Tue. & Thu.-Sat.
❏ Moderate.
An elegant little restaurant with excellent fish dishes, Bandol and Cassis wines, and a cocktail bar (2200-0300).

HÔTEL-RESTAURANT CORNICHE 1 Littoral Frédéric Mistral.
❏ 1200-1430 Tue.-Sat., 1900-2130 Tue.-Fri. ❏ Moderate.
Rustic Provençal décor. Good-value prix-fixe menus and wine.

MADELEINE 7 rue des Tombades.
❏ 1215-1445 Thu.-Tue., 1915-2145 Thu.-Mon. ❏ Moderate.
Best-value cuisine in town. The bourride (fish soup) is recommended.

LA CALANQUE 25 rue Denfert Rochereau.
❏ 1200-1415, 1915-2130 Tue.-Sun. ❏ Moderate.
A small restaurant popular with local businessmen; good fish dishes.

LE DAUPHIN 21 bis rue Jean Jaurès.
❏ 1200-1415 Mon.-Fri., 1915-2115 Mon.-Sat. ❏ Moderate.
Nouvelle cuisine Provençal style, including roast lamb and olives, and sole in crayfish sauce.

RINY 52 rue Jean Jaurès.
❏ 1200-1330 Fri.-Wed., 1900-2200 Mon.-Wed., Fri. & Sat.
❏ Inexpensive.
Watch the chef at work in the kitchen. His speciality is coq au vin.

LE MONARQUE 2 bis Pl. Gambetta.
❏ 1200-1400, 1900-2215 Wed.-Mon. ❏ Inexpensive.
Amazing hors d'oeuvre – they have up to 20 varieties!

Accidents & Breakdowns: Motorists involved in a traffic accident must complete a *constat à l'amiable* before the vehicle is moved. If the vehicle has been seriously damaged, an expert's examination is advised prior to your return to the UK. The *constat à l'amiable* was introduced by the French insurance companies and represents the European Accident Statement Form. It must be signed by the other party, but if a dispute arises and one of the parties involved refuses to complete it, then the other party should immediately obtain a written report from a bailiff (*huissier*), which is known as a *constat d'huissier*. A bailiff can usually be found in any large town and charges a fee of 400F for preparing the report. Normally the police are only called out to accidents when persons are injured, a driver is under the influence of alcohol, or the accident impedes traffic flow. If your vehicle breaks down, obtain local assistance as there is no countrywide motoring club road service in France. For assistance on a motorway, telephone the *brigade de gendarmerie* from an emergency telephone or service station. The police will contact a garage for you, but should it be necessary to remove the vehicle from the motorway for repair, the choice of garage can be determined by the motorist. For AA members there is an emergency service, tel: 05302222 or 21872121. For RAC members, tel: 21963530 and for motorists covered by a Europ Assistance policy, tel: 19-4416801234. The AA has a port service in Calais, Boulogne and Cherbourg. See **Consulates**, **Driving**, **Emergency Numbers**, **Insurance**.

Accommodation: Hotels – there are five categories: * (basic), **
(comfortable), *** (very comfortable), **** (high class) and ***** (luxury). A double room costs anything between 150F and 1500F per night.
The cheaper, more basic hotels are usually near the railway and bus
stations. You will find booking facilities at the main tourist offices in
each town. They offer help with last-minute difficulties, but not neces-
sarily the best deal. The youth hostel (see **A-Z**) in each main town offers
economic lodgings. See **Camping & Caravanning**, **Holiday Villages**,
Tourist Information.

Airports: The Riviera has one major airport, Nice Côte d'Azur, 7 km
west of the town centre and easily reached by taxi, Bus 9 or Air France
buses along the N 89. Airport bus stops in Nice are in Pl. Masséna and
by the port. Nice airport serves four million passengers annually and is
large and sophisticated, with banks, currency exchange facilities, medical services, car-rental desks, restaurants and bars. Flights leave fre-
quently to Paris, London, New York and many other destinations. Air
France and British Airways both fly direct to London. The Air France
office is at 7 Ave Gustave V, tel: 93839101. For flight information,
tel: 93213030. There are minor airports at Toulon/Hyères (Hyères-
Plage, 21 km east of Toulon); St. Raphaël/Fréjus (2 km south of Fréjus,
between the N 98 and the sea); Cannes/Mandelieu (St. Cassien,
between the A 8 and the N 98); and a heliport at Fontvieille, Monaco.

Antibes

Antibes: Pop: 64,000. 11 km northeast of Cannes. Tourist information: 12 Pl. du Général de Gaulle. Originally a Greek trading post in the 4thC BC, Antibes was known during this time as Antipolis. In the 14th-15thC, it became a fortress town on the border between the lands of the dukes of Savoy who held Nice, and the king of France, who had purchased the town from the Grimaldi (see **A-Z**). During 1794 Napoleon (see **A-Z**) lived here with his family. The *vieille ville*, flower markets in cours Masséna, cathedral, Musée Picasso, Port Vauban, Fort Carré and sea ramparts nowadays make Antibes an attractive resort. To the southeast is the beautiful Cap d'Antibes with a footpath around it, and to the southwest exuberant Juan-les-Pins. See **ANTIBES**.

Artisan Centres: There are 50 towns and villages producing a wide variety of handicraft products, particularly *céramique faïence* and *poterie*. There are also artisans making elaborate *bougies* (candles), *vannerie* (basketwork), *bois d'olivier* (olive-wood objects), *taille de pierre* (stone carvings), *travail de cuir* (leatherware), *tapisserie* (tapestry), *tissage* (weaving) and *peinture sur soie* (silk-screen printing). A number of villages in the Var are particularly interesting: Cogolin, Salernes, Le Castellet, Bormes-les-Mimosas, Le Val, Draguignan (see **A-Z**) and Aigunes. *Santons* are clay figures of 'little saints' about 45 cm high, and are a delightful speciality of the region. They are made at Cabris and Tourrettes-sur-Loup, but are on sale in every large Riviera town. See **Best Buys**.

Baby-sitters: Ask your hotel manager if any of the chambermaids are prepared to baby-sit. In Nice the Association Niçoise de Services, 19 Ave Nôtre-Dame, tel: 93805200, provides baby-sitters. Tourist offices can also recommend agencies offering this service. See **Children**.

Bandol: Pop: 6700. 17 km west of Toulon. Tourist information: allées Vivien. This most westerly resort town of the Riviera is rather sophisticated, with a casino, three sandy coves, a lively fishing and yacht harbour with an elegant tree-lined promenade, hotels, restaurants and cafés. There are several discos and piano bars. Local attractions include the Jardin Exotique et Parc Zoologique (0900-1800; 40F), 3 km north beyond the autoroute, the Circuit Paul Ricard motor-racing track, 18 km north, just off the N 8 near Le Beausset, visits to the offshore islands of Île de Bendor and Île des Embiez (see **Islands**), and the local vineyards, which produce fruity red wines (see **A-Z**). There are plenty of restaurants, including Les Oliviers, Bd L. Lumière, La Grotte Provençal, rue Docteur Marçon and Auberge du Port, 9 allée Jean Moulin. See **TOULON-EXCURSIONS**.

Banks: See **Currency**, **Money**, **Opening Times**.

Bardot, Brigitte (1934-): The well-known French actress put St. Tropez (see **A-Z**) on the map in the mid-1950s as a glamorous resort for the young and beautiful. She still owns a villa there.

Beaulieu-sur-Mer: Pop 4300. 10 km northeast of Nice. Tourist information: Pl. de la Gare. A small, sheltered, fashionable resort with a large marina, casino and many handsome Edwardian villas. The luxuriant gardens and palm trees have caused the town to be nicknamed Petite Afrique, a result of the subtropical climate with which it is blessed. Restaurants include the well-known Metropole and La Reserve, both in Bd Maréchal Leclerc and both expensive, and Les Agaves, rue Maréchal Foch and La Pignatelle, 10 rue de Quincenet, which are smaller and have reasonable prices. See **NICE-EXCURSION 2**.

Best Buys: The Riviera towns have a vast array of chic and usually expensive shops. Unusual presents include a bottle or two of the local wine (for instance, Bellet of Nice – see **Wines**), olive oil, olive-oil soaps, beautiful candles, olive-wood sculptures, silk prints, *santons*, stained glass, enamel tiles, puppets, murals, handmade jewellery, glasswork and dried flowers, and, from many villages, ceramics and pottery. Perfumes from Grasse (see **A-Z**) are widely distributed, while some of the local markets have stalls selling unusual foods. See **Artisan Centres**, **Shopping**.

Bicycle & Motorcycle Hire: Several SNCF stations will rent you bicycles, i.e. Antibes, Juan-les-Pins, St. Raphaël, Hyères, Digne, Bandol, Cagnes-sur-Mer and Cannes. Expect to pay a substantial deposit for bikes, scooters, mopeds or motorcycles, plus a daily charge. There are reduced rates for three-day and weekly rentals. Comprehensive insurance is recommended, as well as a protective helmet.
Main hiring outlets:
Cannes: Deux Roues Location, 5 rue Alleis; Menton: Europcar, 9 Ave Thiers; Monaco: Auto-Moto Garage, 7 rue de la Colle; Nice: Nicea Location Rent, 9 Ave Thiers and Ets Arnaud, 4 Pl. Grimaldi; St. Tropez: Mas Louis, 5 rue Joseph Quaranta.

Biot: Pop: 3750. 8 km northwest of Antibes. Tourist information: Pl. Chapelle. A small village which is well worth a visit to see the rose, carnation and mimosa cultivation, plus the pottery and ceramic artisans, glassworks (Novarro in particular) and Musée Fernand Léger (1000-1200, 1400-1700 Wed.-Mon.; 12F). The museum has over 300 of the artist's (see **Léger**) cubist works on display, including canvases, ceramics, stained glass, mosaics, sculptures and machines. Reliable restaurants are Café des Arcades, 16 Pl. des Arcades and Auberge du Jarrier, Pl. Chapelle.

Boat Trips: All the offshore islands, including Île de Lérins, Îles d'Hyères and Corsica, can be visited from Nice and Toulon. The main ferry company is SNCM, 3 Ave Gustave V, Nice and 21-49 Ave de l'Infanterie de Marine, Toulon. The *gare maritime* is the focal point for ferry arrivals and departures. In addition, local boats ply between St. Tropez and St. Raphaël, Menton and Monaco. Fares during the period Oct.-May are lower but sailings are fewer. Discounts are available for the over-60s and the under-26s. See **Islands**.

Braque, Georges (1882-1963): The founder, with Picasso (see **A-Z**), of cubism in art. He spent his last years painting in Le Cannet, near Cannes. Fondation Maeght near St. Paul-de-Vence (see **A-Z**) has a number of his mosaics, canvases and drawings.

SERVICE des ILES de LÉRINS

Ste. Marguerite   St. Honorat

Visite de la Corniche d'Or
COMPAGNIE ESTÉREL CHANTECLAIR / 93 39 11 82

Cannes

Biot

Budget: The Riviera has a reputation for being expensive. If you stay at the Negresco (see **NICE-ATTRACTIONS**), the Carlton at Cannes, or the Paris or Hermitage in Monte-Carlo, this is indeed true and the sky is the limit. However, there are hundreds of moderately-priced hotels and restaurants for travellers with more limited means.

Hotel bedroom for two	175F-3000F
Petit déjeuner (breakfast)	35F-200F
Three-course lunch or dinner	75F-1000F
Carafe of wine in a bistro	25F-40F
Museum entry fee	12F-25F
Soft drink in a café	10F-25F
Picnic lunch from a supermarket	40F-80F

Buses: An excellent mode of transport both locally and from the *gares routières* (bus stations) for longer journeys. Carnets of five tickets offer discounts.

Main bus stations:
Antibes: rue de la République; Cannes: Quai St. Pierre and Pl. de
l'Hôtel de Ville; Menton: Ave de Sospel; Nice: 131 Promenade du
Paillon; St. Tropez: Ave du 8 Mai; Toulon: Bd Commandant Nicolas.

Cagnes-sur-Mer: Pop: 35,500. 13 km southwest of Nice. Tourist
information: 26 Ave Auguste Renoir. Three major roads trisect the
town, but just inland are the more attractive villages of Cagnes-Ville,
Haut-de-Cagnes and Villeneuve-Loubet. The last two are situated on
hills and have been popular with artists for over a century. Musée
Renoir du Souvenir (1000-1200, 1400-1800; 20F) in Les Collettes,
Cagnes-Ville is where the artist (see **Renoir**) spent the last years of his
life. The Château-Musée (1000-1200, 1400-1800; 10F), Haut-de-
Cagnes is used in summer for the international art festival (July-Sep.;
20F) and also contains the unusual Musée de l'Olivier (of the Olive
Tree) and Musée d'Art Méditerranéen Moderne, both of which are
worth seeing. Good restaurants are Le Cagnard, rue du Pontis Long and
Les Peintres, 71 montée de la Bourgade, both in Haut-de-Cagnes. See
NICE-EXCURSION 1.

Cameras & Photography: Films, video cassettes and flashes are
widely available in all towns. Check with staff before using a camera in
museums or art galleries, as there are usually restrictions.

Camping & Caravanning: There are over 300 camp sites in the
departments of the Var and Alpes Maritimes. There are four categories
for price and amenities. Prices for one- and two-star sites are strictly
controlled but three- and four-star sites operate in a 'free' market. This
means that the nearer the site is to the coast, the higher the price.
Conversely, many inland sites are remarkably inexpensive. Many sites
only open May-Oct. Lower rates are charged for out-of-season months.
Many sites also require booking in advance. The French Government
Tourist Office, 178 Piccadilly, London W1 can supply a list of sites recommended by the Touring Club de France. For camping on farmland,
contact Fédération Nationale des Gîtes Ruraux de France, 35 rue
Godot-de-Maurey, Paris 75009.

Cannes: Pop: 72,800. 33 km southwest of Nice. Tourist information: Palais des Festivals et des Congrès, Bd de la Croisette and SNCF, 1 rue Jean Jaurès. This, the smartest and most sophisticated of the Riviera towns, was founded by Lord Brougham, a British ex-chancellor. An outbreak of cholera in Nice in 1834 forced him to halt here and he thought the place so enchanting – it was then a small fishing village – that he built a villa and wintered in Cannes for the next 34 years. His aristocratic friends and royalty followed suit. Splendid hotels were built on the 3 km-long Bd de la Croisette overlooking the beach. Streets are still named Victoria, Roi Albert I, Prince-de-Galles, Oxford and Albert Edward. Cannes' festivals are well known – the International Film Festival, Mideni (Records and Music), IMTP (Television) – and along with the various regattas the year is a nonstop stream of 'attractions'. The town can boast a marina, *gare maritime*, casino, observatory, several museums, and an abundance of ultra-chic boutiques and exclusive hotels and restaurants set in superb gardens with palm trees and subtropical plants. A fee is charged for entry to 20 of the beaches, of which Maschou and Carlton are the most up-market, but there is one free section at the west end of the town. The best shopping centres are rue Meynadier, Bd de la Croisette and rue d'Antibes, as well as the Hôtel Gray d'Albion galleries on rue des Serbes. See **CANNES**.

Cap-Ferrat: See **NICE-EXCURSION 2**.

Car Hire: To hire a car you must produce a passport and a current driving licence which has been valid for at least one year. A cash deposit is necessary unless paying by credit card, and also proof of a local (hotel) address. The minimum age is 21-25, depending on the company. Be sure to check the basis of charge, i.e. a daily rate plus so much per km or unlimited mileage. Third-party insurance is compulsory. Avis, Hertz and Europcar have car-rental facilities in every large Riviera town and at Toulon/Hyères, Nice Côte d'Azur and Cannes/Mandelieu airports. Local firms are usually cheaper and often just as reliable.

Casinos: Gamblers can try their luck at chemin de fer, roulette, baccarat, etc., and on the ubiquitous one-armed bandits, in casinos which are usually situated on the seafront. The two in Nice lead a haphazard existence – sometimes open, often not! Monte-Carlo also has two – the Casino de Monte-Carlo and Loews/SBM – with American gaming rules. Besides the gambling facility, most casinos have a restaurant and a dance floor or disco. An entrance fee is usually required to gamble in the *salles privées*. You may be asked for proof of identity and that you are over 21. See the **NIGHTLIFE** topic pages for **ANTIBES, CANNES, MONACO, NICE** and **ST. TROPEZ**.

Chagall, Marc (1887-1985): The Russian surrealist painter whose later years were spent in Vence (see **A-Z**). In 1948 he settled permanently on the Côte d'Azur and in 1972 set up the Musée National Marc Chagall (see **NICE-MUSEUMS 1**), where several hundred of his paintings, gouaches and mosaics, including *Message Biblique*, can be seen. His brilliant glass mosaics can also be seen in St. Roseline's chapel at Les Arcs.

Chemists: Chemists (*pharmacies*) can be identified by their green cross signs and will be found in every Riviera town. They all have a list in the window giving addresses of late-night and Sun. openings. See **Health, Opening Times**.

Children: As well as swimming, canoe/kayak trips, tennis and walking, there are zoos at Monaco, Bandol, St. Jean-Cap-Ferrat and Toulon, the huge Zoo Marin (see **ANTIBES-ATTRACTIONS**), and two safari parks near Fréjus (see **A-Z**). Some museums may also be of interest: Musée Oceanographique et Aquarium (see **MONACO-MUSE-UMS**); Musée des Papillons (butterflies) (1600-1900 Wed.-Sun., May-Sep.; 12F) at Levens, 20 km north of Nice; Musée National des Poupées et des Automates (see **MONACO-MUSEUMS**); and Musée Historial des Princes de Monaco (see **MONACO-MUSEUMS**). The Parc des Miniatures (see **NICE-PARKS & GARDENS**) has a huge array of models of towns and harbours, and people from the Middle Ages right up to the present day, on a scale of 1:25 – a child's delight. The OK Corral (0900-2100 Mar.-Oct.; 50F), on the N 8 17 km north of Bandol, has attractions on a Western theme, including stagecoaches, ranches and shoot-outs, for children of all ages! See **Baby-sitters**.

Climate: Apart from the occasional appearance of the cold mistral wind blowing down the Rhône valley and around St. Tropez, and the sirocco wind from Africa, the French Riviera has the most equable climate in France, perhaps in Europe. Frost, fog and snow are rare and spring sees the subtropical flowers and vegetation at their best, helped by brief rainstorms. Summer temperatures are an average of 22°C , but the sea breezes keep the conditions comfortable. There are occasional violent storms in autumn but, as in spring, the Mediterranean flowers bloom again.

Cocteau, Jean (1889-1963): A poet, painter, film maker and dramatist, he had a summer home at Cap Ferrat (see **NICE-EXCURSION 2**). See his fishing and harlequin murals in Musée Jean Cocteau (see **MENTON-ATTRACTIONS**), Chapelle St. Pierre in Villefranche-sur-Mer and a sundial in Coaraze.

Complaints: It is unusual on the French Riviera to be overcharged in hotels or restaurants, but nevertheless you should check every bill as you would at home. Ensure that if you have chosen a fixed-price menu (there may be several), the waiter knows which one you have selected. Taxis may take you by a longer route than is strictly necessary! If you have a serious complaint take it immediately to the manager of the establishment. If you get no satisfaction go to the local tourist information office and only as a final resort go to the police (see **A-Z**). See **Tourist Information**.

Consulates:
UK – 11 rue Paradis, 06000 Nice, tel: 93823204.
USA – 31 rue du Maréchal Joffre, 06000 Nice, tel: 93888955.

Conversion Chart:

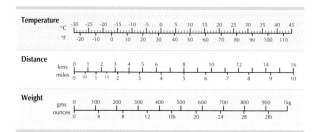

Corniches: The three parallel coast roads linking Nice, Monaco and
Menton, from which there are spectacular views of the Mediterranean,
are known as corniches (cliff-side roads). The upper or Grande
Corniche is the D 2564; the middle or Moyenne Corniche is the N 7;
and the lower or Basse Corniche is the N 98. In July and Aug. they are
full to overflowing with traffic. Technically, the A 8 autoroute from Aix-
en-Provence to the Italian border is the newest and highest corniche.
See **Driving**.

Credit Cards: See **Money**.

Crime & Theft: Never leave your car unlocked for even a short
time, and be sure to remove or hide any valuables. If you do have anything stolen, report the theft immediately to the nearest police station
(*commissariat de police*) and obtain an *attestation de vol* document so
that you can claim insurance. You must inform your consulate (see **A-Z**)
at once if your passport is stolen. See **Emergency Numbers**, **Insurance**,
Police.

Currency: The French unit of currency is the franc, which divides into 100 centimes. Banknotes are issued for 500F, 200F, 100F, 50F and 20F. Coins are 10F (two types, the older version is bronze-coloured, the newer ones are smaller with a brass rim and silver centre), 5F, 2F, 1F, 50c (all silver), 20c, 10c and 5c (all brass). See **Money**.

Customs Allowances:

Duty Paid Into:	Cigarettes	*or* Cigars	*or* Tobacco	Spirits	Wine
E C	300	75	400 g	1.5 *l*	5 *l*
U K	300	75	400 g	1.5 *l*	5 *l*

Disabled People: For information about accommodation, transport, facilities and aids for the disabled, see the booklets *Touristes Quand Même* and *Guide des Transports à l'Usage des Personnes à Mobilité Réduite*, supplied by the tourist office. All TGV high-speed trains can

accommodate wheelchairs, and guide dogs are transported free. Other trains have a special compartment and an escalator for boarding. See **Health**, **Tourist Information**.

Draguignan: Pop: 28,200. 65 km west of Cannes. Tourist information: 9 Bd Clemenceau. The name of this handsome old market town, inland from Fréjus, derives from a 5thC dragon that terrified passing pilgrims! The old marketplace, 13thC synagogue, 17thC clock tower and the Flemish and

Italian paintings in the interesting Musée Municipal (1000-1200 Tue.-Sat., 1400-1800 Mon.-Sat.; 12F) make Draguignan worth a visit. The American war cemetery, where nearly a thousand soldiers are buried, killed as a result of the 1944 invasion (see **World War II**), is 2 km east on the D 59. Notable restaurants in the town include Les Pignatelles, rte de Bagnols and Les Deux Cochers, 7 Bd G. Péri.

Drinks: In France there are no licensing laws, so you can buy alcohol in bars and cafés at any time. House wines are sold by the litre (*une carafe*), half litre (*un demi-litre*) or quarter litre (*un quart*); a jug (*un pichet*) can hold either a quarter or half litre. Beer is usually lager. At meals plain water (*une carafe d'eau*) comes free. Coffee: ask for *un café* for a small strong black espresso, *un café au lait* for coffee with milk and *un grand crème* for a large white coffee. Tea is available at *salons de thé* and hot chocolate is popular: ask for *un chocolat*. Drinks are less expensive served standing in a bar or café (*au comptoir*) than seated. A pavement table may cost a great deal more. See **Wines**.

Driving: Rush-hour traffic in the big towns and driving along the corniches (see **A-Z**) in high season are not for the inexperienced driver.
You will need a valid national or international driving licence plus
comprehensive insurance documents (preferably a Green Card), nation-
ality sticker, yellow filters for headlamps and a red warning triangle.
The French drive on the right-hand side of the road, and at T-junctions,
intersections and roundabouts the traffic from the right has priority. The
wearing of seat belts is compulsory for passengers in the front and recommended for those in the back. Try to make long journeys by car on
Sun. when trucks are forbidden by law. Speed limits: built-up areas
60 kph; main roads 90-110 kph; motorways (autoroutes) 130 kph.
Speeding offences carry a large on-the-spot fine from the motorway
police. There are emergency telephones approximately every 20 km on
main roads. These are connected direct to the local police stations
which operate 24 hr. In larger towns emergency help is available from
the Police Secours (Emergency Assistance Department). NOTE: French
drivers are very competitive and a foreign numberplate is a challenge
to them which should be resisted. See **Accidents & Breakdowns**, **Car
Hire**, **Emergency Numbers**, **Parking**, **Petrol**.

Drugs: In France it is illegal to use or possess any form of narcotic,
and anyone caught trying to smuggle drugs into the country faces
almost certain imprisonment.

Eating Out: By law all restaurants must display their prices outside
and have at least one fixed-price menu (*menu fixe*, *rapide menu*, *menu
touristique*), as well as the à la carte. These fixed-price menus for two
or three courses can cost as little as 65F, whereas the à la carte is
always more expensive. The *plat du jour* is usually good, so ask the
waiter what it is. Restaurants traditionally serve lunch from 1200 and
rarely after 1400, and the evening meal from 1930-2100, but
brasseries, bistros and *le drugstore* will serve a *plat du jour* at almost
any time. Cafés serve a variety of drinks all day, as well as snacks,
sandwiches and *croque-monsieur* (a toasted ham and cheese sand-
wich). Every tourist office will have a list of local restaurants, with
addresses, telephone numbers, style of cuisine and some indication of

price. On the **RESTAURANTS** topic pages of this guide, an Inexpensive meal would cost 50F-100F, a Moderate meal 100F-200F and an Expensive meal over 200F. See the **RESTAURANTS** topic pages for **ANTIBES, CANNES, MENTON, MONACO, NICE, ST. TROPEZ** and **TOULON, Food**.

Electricity: The voltage in France is 220 V and a two-pin adaptor is required, available from most electrical shops.

Emergency Numbers:

Police	17
Fire brigade (*sapeurs-pompiers*)	18
SAMU (24 hr ambulance):	
Antibes	93334020
Cannes	93383938
Menton	93414141
Monaco	93259900
Nice	93925555 or 93830101
St. Tropez	94976555
Toulon	94270707

Events:

January: Monaco, feast of St. Dévote at La Condamine; Monte-Carlo car rally.

February: Cannes, Corso of the Mimosa; Nice, Bataille des Fleurs, fireworks and processions. *Shrove Tuesday:* Menton, Corso of the Golden Fruit (lemons), procession, floats; Nice, Corso du Mardi Gras.

March: Nice, Fête des Cougardons (pumpkins) in Cimiez arena.

Easter Sunday: Vence, Bataille des Fleurs, Provençal song and dance.

April: Toulon, Hyères, Bormes-les-Mimosas, flower parades.

May: Cannes, International Film Festival; Nice, Fête des Mais in Cimiez gardens, with dancing round the maypole under the olive trees; Grasse, Festival of the Roses; St. Tropez, Bravade de St. Torpes, folk festival; Monaco Grand Prix, Formula 1 car race.

June: Hyères, St. Tropez, Brignoles, folklore festivals (*bravades*).

July: Nice, jazz and folklore festivals in Cimiez arena; Juan-les-Pins/Antibes, World Jazz Festival; Toulon, International Dance Festival; *Bastille Day:* Fireworks and processions everywhere on the 14th.

August: Grasse, jasmine and folklore festivals; Nice, Bataille des Fleurs; Menton, Chamber Music Festival.

September: Cannes, Royal Regatta; Nice, Fête de la Vigne (wine festival) in Cimiez arena.

November: Toulon, *santon* fair; Nice, two-day motor rally.

Èze: Pop: 2100. 12 km northeast of Nice. Tourist information: La Mairie (Town Hall). A spectacular hill village with Jardin Exotique, castle and many artisan shops on the Moyenne Corniche 400 m above the Mediterranean, from where there are superb views across to Corsica. See **NICE-EXCURSION 2**.

Food: The wide variety of locally-grown vegetables and herbs, particularly tomatoes, aubergines, olives and garlic, ensures colourful dishes such as *salade niçoise*, *tapenade*, *crudités*, *aioli* and ratatouille are always available. Every fishing harbour lands a vast array of fish such as *loup* (sea bass), sardines, anchovies, *rascasse*, *rouget* (red mullet), *daurade* (John Dory) and shellfish – lobster, crab, prawns and *écrevisses* (crayfish). Bouillabaisse and *bourride* are both tasty fish dishes, and can be washed down with the local wines (see **A-Z**) of Bandol, St. Tropez and Bellet. Two local cheeses are *banon*, wrapped in chestnut leaves, and *cachal* (sheep's milk marinated with herbs). A morning visit to the local markets (see **A-Z**) to see the freshly-caught fish, colourful vegetables and delicious fruit will certainly be rewarding. See **Eating Out**.

Forest Fires: Every summer these are a major hazard, usually caused by picnickers or drivers who are careless with cigarettes. Be especially alert when driving between Toulon and Nice. See **Emergency Numbers**.

Fragonard, Jean Honoré (1732-1806): A Romantic painter born in Grasse, he worked in Paris in the studios of Boucher and David. Some of his works can be seen in the Villa-Musée Fragonard and cathedral in Grasse. The Maison Fragonard in Bd Fragonard is the Grasse perfume factory, which also houses a small scent museum. See **Grasse**.

Fréjus: Pop: 32,700. 40 km southwest of Cannes. Tourist information: Pl. Calvini. Founded in 49 BC by Julius Caesar, and originally called Forum Julii, Fréjus became an important port with a population of 25,000. The episcopal complex comprising a 5thC octagonal baptistry, 10th-12thC Gothic cathedral, 13thC cloister and museum is certainly worth exploring. The 30 min guided tour (1000-1200, 1400-1800 Wed.-Mon., April-Sep.; 20F) can be booked at 48 rue de Fleury. Also see the *cité Romaine* with its theatre and ramparts, and an arena which is still occasionally used for bullfights. Fréjus-Plage is 1.5 km southeast of the town centre and has 5 km of sandy beach, merging into St. Raphaël (see **A-Z**). Fréjus' Parc Zoologique and Safari de l'Esterel (0900-2100; 45F, child 25F) are 5 km northwest on the D 4. Recommended restaurants include Le Vieux Four, 46 rue Grisolle, Lou Calen, 9 rue Desaugiers and Le Caquelon, rue Pie Bertagna.

Garibaldi, Giuseppe (1807-82): Born in Quai Lunel, Port Lympia, Nice, the instigator of Italian Unification in 1860 and great Franco-Italian patriot is remembered in Nice by Pl. Garibaldi (see **NICE-ATTRACTIONS**) which contains his statue. Displays on Garibaldi can be seen in Musée Masséna (see **NICE-MUSEUMS 1**).

Grasse: Pop: 38,360. 17 km northwest of Cannes. Tourist information: Pl. de la Foux. Once a tiny medieval republic trading with Italy in scented gloves and soaps, since the 18thC Grasse has been world-renowned for its perfumes. Thirty factories, including Fragonard and Molinard, produce 90% of the world's flower essence for scents,

derived from roses, jasmine, violet, orange blossom, mimosa and lavender. The *vieille ville,* with the 12th-17thC Cathédrale de Nôtre-Dame-du-Puy containing paintings by Ruberei and Fragonard (see **A-Z**), Pl. du Cours, Pl. aux Aires and rue de Fontette (all with picturesque alleyways and houses), is well worth a visit. Grasse has four museums: Musée Amiral de Grasse (1000-1200, 1400-1800 Tue.-Sun., Dec.-Oct.; 10F), Hôtel de Ponteves, Bd du Jeu de Ballon, a naval museum devoted to the career and exploits of the famous French admiral (1722-88); Musée d'Art et d'Histoire (times and admission as above), 2 rue Mirabeau, a folklore museum showing Provençal life and traditions; Villa-Musée Fragonard (times and admission as above), 23 Bd Fragonard, where the painter was born and showing works of art by the Fragonard family; and Maison Fragonard (0900-1200, 1400-1800 Mon.-Sat.; free), 20 Bd Fragonard, a commercial perfume factory with a small scent museum. Recommended restaurants in the town include Maître Boscq, 13 rue de Fontette, Chez Pierre, 3 Ave Thiers and Amphitryon, 16 Bd Victor Hugo. See **NICE-EXCURSION 1**.

Grimaldi: Originally from Genoa, this powerful family has ruled the principality of Monaco since the 16thC, although François Grimaldi first captured it in 1297. Prince Rainier III is the present ruler.

Grimaud & Port-Grimaud: Pop· 5000. 10 km west of St. Tropez. Tourist information: Bd des Aliziers. The former is a small dignified hill town with a castle, 11thC Templar church and medieval streets overlooking the Golfe de St. Tropez. The latter is a modern marina, a charming but controversial re-creation of a Provençal fishing village, built in the 1960s with Venetian-style canals, bridges, alleyways and beaches but no roads. Restaurants in Port-Grimaud include La Marina at Le Port and La Tartane, Pl. du 14 Juin, and in the old town, Côteau Fleuri, Pl. des Pénitents and Les Santons, rte Nationale.

Health: Medical treatment through the French social security system is available to all citizens of EC countries. Residents of the UK should obtain form E 111 from the DSS before departure. You will have to pay for any treatment in the first place, then claim it back afterwards. Even an ordinary visit to the doctor costs about 100F, so it certainly pays to take out medical insurance beforehand. Lists of doctors, including those available on Sun. and holidays, can be obtained from police stations, chemists (see **A-Z**) and probably from your hotel. See **Disabled People**, **Emergency Numbers**, **Insurance**.

Hill Villages: Part of the Riviera's charm is the score or more of pretty inland hill villages, usually quiet and attractive oases after the competitive dazzle of the Côte d'Azur resort towns. They are easily reached by car, bus, even train, and every visitor should try to see a couple or more. Èze (see **A-Z**) and Gourdon are quite spectacular with their chateaux, gardens and superb views. St. Paul-de-Vence (see **A-Z**) has its famous museum and painting *ateliers* while Saorge has 15thC houses and a church in a wild countryside setting.

Holiday Villages: These are up-market clusters of chalets, usually near a lake or by the sea, offering a wide variety of loosely-organized activities, including tennis, swimming, riding, cycling, etc. They can be found for example at Heliopolis nudist village on Île du Levant, and on Île de Bendor. Ask the local tourist office for details.

Hyères: Pop: 42,000. 18 km east of Toulon. Tourist information: Pl. Clemenceau. This old Greek trading town on Castéou hill became an inland resort in the 18th and 19thC, visited by Napoleon (see **A-Z**), Queen Victoria, Tolstoy and R. L. Stevenson, and the *vieille ville* with its old streets, churches, parks and gardens is still attractive. You should also try to see the Musée Municipal (0900-1200, 1400-1800 Wed.-Mon.; 12F), with various archaeological finds and works by local artists, in Pl. Lefebvre, and Jardins Olbius Riquier (same hours; 15F), a zoo with a wide range of tropical plants. Recommended restaurants are Le Tisson d'Or, 1 rue Gallieni and Chez Marius, Pl. Massillon. Due south past Toulon/Hyères airport, Port d'Hyères and the racecourse are on one of the two narrow isthmus' leading to the Giens peninsula, which is 11 km south. The peninsula measures 6 km by 1 km, and is a hotchpotch of saltmarsh, seaside resort, fishing ports, fortresses and occasional beaches. See **TOULON-EXCURSIONS**.

Impressionists, The: With its brilliant colours and contrasting light conditions, the Riviera was always popular with the Impressionist School of painters. Nice was host to Berthe Morisot, Matisse (see **A-Z**) and Dufy, Antibes to Monet, Cagnes to Renoir (see **A-Z**), and St. Tropez to Signac (see **A-Z**), Manguin and Bonnard.

Insurance: You should take out comprehensive travel insurance covering you and your family, if travelling with you, against theft and loss of property, car and money, as well as medical expenses, for the duration of your stay. Your travel agent, the AA or RAC will recommend a suitable policy. See **Crime & Theft**, **Driving**, **Health**.

Nice

Islands: There are a number of attractive islands off the Riviera coast, easily reached by ferry from the mainland. From west to east they are: Île de Bendor: Ferry from Bandol. A tiny island owned by the pastis millionaire Paul Ricard. It is now a cultural-tourist centre with a nautical club, wine museum, art gallery, hotels and restaurants. See **TOULON-EXCURSIONS**.

Île des Embiez: Ferry from Bandol or Toulon. A 40 hectare island with a large marina, repair shipyard, marine research centre, museum and aquarium, and a hotel and restaurants owned by Paul Ricard. See **TOULON-EXCURSIONS**.

Îles d'Hyères: Ferry from La Tour Fondue, Toulon, Hyères-Plage and Le Lavandou. A group of three islands of which Porquerolles, 5 km southeast of Giens, has just one village, a church, pine woods, sandy coves, lighthouses and deep seawater *calanques* (creeks). Port-Cros, the middle island, is a heavily-wooded national park. The offshore marine life will be of interest to nature lovers. The hotel-restaurant Le Manoir is near the port in an 18thC manor house. The eastern Hyères island is Levant, which has the nudist village of Heliopolis on its west side; the French navy controls the eastern half. See **TOULON-EXCURSIONS**.

Îles de Lérins: Ferry from Cannes. The two small islands of Ste Marguerite and St. Honorat are thickly wooded and were owned by monks for fourteen centuries. Richelieu's 17thC fort is now a sporting and cultural centre for 14-17 year olds.

Laundries: Hotels will usually do your laundry. All towns along the French Riviera now have self-service, coin-operated Launderettes (*laundromats, laveries automatique*), usually open 0800-1900. In Nice you will find one at 18 rue de Belgique, and in Toulon at 25 rue Baudin.

Léger, Fernand (1881-1955): A cubist painter who lived in Paris but settled in Biot (see **A-Z**). Musée Fernand Léger, southeast of the village, houses nearly 350 of his works.

Lost Property: If you lose anything you should contact the Bureau des Objets Trouvés in any large town.

Marinas: There are a score or more along the coast, at Bandol, Toulon, St. Tropez, St. Raphaël and Villefranche-sur-Mer, plus the well-established ones at Cannes, Monaco and Menton. More recent additions are those at Port-Grimaud, and Port-la-Galère, southwest of Cannes.

Markets: Every town has a covered food market with a wide range of small shops selling meat, cheese, wine, fruit and vegetables. An open market is held on one or two mornings a week and the tourist office will be able to tell you when. The magnificent and colourful range of food will give you clues as to what is on the restaurant menus. Nice and Toulon also have flower, flea and antiques markets. See **Food**, **Tourist Information**.

Matisse, Henri (1869-1954): The leading Fauvist artist first stayed at St. Tropez in 1904 and lived at Cimiez (Nice) and Vence, where he painted odalisques (concubines) and still lifes from 1917 until his death. He also painted in Cassis and the Chapelle du Rosaire at Vence. Musée Matisse (see **NICE-MUSEUMS 1**) is a 'must'.

Maures Massif: This heavily-wooded mountain range runs parallel to the coast for 56 km between Hyères (see **A-Z**) and Fréjus (see **A-Z**), and derives its name from the Provençal word for 'dark' (*maouro*), which perfectly describes the colour of the chestnut, oak and Aleppo pine woods. The highest peak is La Sauvette (780 m) and the range, which extends inland for 20-30 km, is watered by several small rivers, including the Argens, Grimaud, Couloubrier and Gapeau. Wine-bottle corks and delicious *marrons glacés* are made locally.

An attractive one-day excursion starts at Hyères. Drive east for 20 km on the N 98 and D 559 through La-Londe-les-Maures to Le Pin, then inland on the D 41 to the aptly-named village of Bormes-les-Mimosas. From the elegant mimosa and eucalyptus groves there are views out across the Mediterranean. The D 41 winds north for another 20 km across three spectacular passes – Col de Cagoven, Col de Gratteloup and Col de Babaou – to Collobrières. The local *vin rosé* is worth tasting. From the village you could take a detour east for 6 km to the Charterhouse of La Verna (1100-1900 Wed.-Mon., Nov.-Sep.; 20F), a Carthusian monastery founded in 1170. Return to the D 14 and continue east for 25 km to Grimaud (see **A-Z**), then go south on the D 558 for 3 km to Cogolin where a number of crafts are practised (see **Artisan Centres**). Follow the N 98 to La Foux, then take the D 559 to Gassin, which is perched on a small hill, from where there are superb views stretching from the bay of St. Tropez to the Îles d'Hyères. The return to Hyères is via the beautiful Corniche des Maures (D 559) and the attractive little resorts of La Croix-Valmer, Le Rayol, Canadel-sur-Mer, Pramousquier, Cavalière, Aigue-la-Belle and St. Clair, and the charming Le Lavandou, where Au Vieux Port and La Bouée are both reliable restaurants. NOTE: Watch out for forest fires in midsummer, and be extremely careful with cigarettes.

Menton: 10 km northeast of Monaco. Pop: 25,500. Tourist information: Palais de l'Europe, Jardins de Biovès and Promenade du Soleil. The prettiest, warmest and friendliest of all the Riviera resorts. On the French/Italian border, backed by terraces crammed with olive and citrus trees, Menton was very popular with the European nobility in the 19th and early 20thC. Two marinas, long sandy beaches, a casino, several tropical gardens and two interesting museums make Menton a pleasant place to visit. In particular, visit Parvis St. Michel on the hill in the *vieille ville*, from where there are views of the Italian Riviera and the yachts in the harbour. The famous lemon festival in Feb. and the chamber music festival in Aug. are the town's two main events. See **MENTON**.

Monaco: 18 km east of Nice. Tourist information: 2 Bd des Moulins. This must be the most famous principality in the world. The Grimaldi (see **A–Z**) captured Monaco in 1297, 'purchased' it officially in 1308 and it became a principality in the 16thC. Now with 200 hectares and a population of 27,000 (4500 Monegasque), it looks like a more glamorous (tax concession) version of Hong Kong. From west to east there are four separate areas. Fontvieille has recently been reclaimed from the sea and is entirely man-made, with a marina and many Provençal-coloured apartment blocks with shops and boutiques at ground level. The noisy heliport is next door to a new park, the Princess Grace rose garden, and the brand-new Louis II sports stadium. Next are the Palais Princier, cathedral, museums and *vieille ville*, situated on top of a very

large rock, and known as Monaco-Ville. To the east is the major marina-port and not-so-glamorous town of La Condamine, and beyond, to the east of another large spur, is Monte-Carlo, with its fine hotels, casinos, gardens, theatre and top-quality shopping. There are 33 different banks, some with half a dozen branches, since Monaco is a major tax haven and French, British, American and Swiss banks compete vigorously with nine Monegasque banks for offshore funds. Despite the Manhattan skyscraper effect, this little country has many beautiful tropical gardens, spotlessly clean streets, and an almost complete lack of crime, a situation encouraged by the handsome white-capped *agents de police*. Of course, there are certain 'musts': try (within your means!) to break the bank of Monte-Carlo at one of the three gambling establishments; watch the changing of the guard outside the palace; visit the old town with its narrow streets, restaurants, artisans and some inevitable tawdry junk; and have a drink at the outside tables of the Café de Paris and watch the world go by. In summer, swimming in the relatively clean Mediterranean is possible from the horseshoe-shaped beach at Le Larvotto. In the evening you may wish to visit one of the dozen or so nightclubs and discreet piano bars. There are a score or more superb restaurants but you may have to seek out the truly Monegasque specialities – *barbaguian* (mixed vegetables, rice and cheese), *stocafe* (stockfish casserole with black olives, onions, tomatoes, potatoes, wine and cognac) and *fugassa de munega* (cake with rum, raisins, aniseed, nuts and almonds). Parking is extremely difficult but there are 22 official car parks, many recently built underground. All in all, Monaco is an exciting, interesting (and safe) independent state with nonstop entertainment throughout the year. See **MONACO**.

Money: Every large town has a wide choice of banks. There are exchange facilities at airports and main-line railway stations, as well as in most tourist offices (useful at weekends), some hotels and travel agencies. Most main post offices (see **A–Z**) have currency exchange facilities, often with a low rate of commission. Cities have a number of bureaux de change in the centre and near the SNCF. Exchange rates and commission charges vary, so it pays to look around. Credit cards are widely accepted, with Visa (Carte Bleue) being the most common.

Traveller's cheques are probably the safest way to carry holiday money and can be used in many locations but not in smaller hotels and restaurants. They are easy to change at any bank or bureau de change. See **Currency**.

Mougins: Pop: 12,000. 8 km north of Cannes. Tourist information: Ave J. Ch. Mallet. A fortified hill-top town with ramparts, narrow alleyways and restored houses. Visit the Musée de l'Automobile de Mougins (1000-1900; 30F), a collection of 70 vintage cars which is situated 5 km northwest on the D 235 and D 3. Of the town's eight good restaurants Moulin de Mougins, in a 16thC olive-oil mill in the hamlet of Nôtre-Dame de Vie, 2 km east on the D 3, and Ferme de Mougins at 10 Ave St. Basile are superb but expensive. See **NICE-EXCURSION 1**.

Music: Festivals of music, drama and dance are held each year at Nice, Menton, Cannes and Grasse, and jazz festivals at Juan-les-Pins and Nice. Monte-Carlo, Nice and Toulon have opera seasons (see **NICE-NIGHTLIFE**) as well as performances by their own orchestras. See **Events**, **Tourist Information**.

Napoleon Bonaparte (1769-1821): The little Corsican has several links with the Riviera. He first won fame at the siege of Toulon in 1793, and the following year he lived with his family as a young general in command of coastal defences in Antibes. When he was forced to abdicate in 1814 he sailed from St. Raphaël to exile on Elba. However, in 1815 he returned and landed at Golfe-Juan with 800 men. He marched north by the Route Napoléon – the modern N 85 – to Grenoble and Paris, via Antibes, Cannes, Grasse, Digne and Sisteron. The small Musée Napoléon (see **MONACO-MUSEUMS**) in the Palais Princier in Monaco-Ville contains some Napoleonic souvenirs.

Newspapers: English newspapers are available, usually by early afternoon, in *librairies* (book and newspaper shops) and some kiosks in the major Riviera towns.

Nice: Pop: 340,000. 18 km west of Monaco, 956 km south of Paris. Tourist information: Ave Thiers, Palais des Congrès, Esplanade Kennedy, and 5 Ave Gustave V. Colonized by the Greeks in the 4thC BC, the capital of the Côte d'Azur has a superb natural setting and climate that make it a most attractive city, the fifth-largest in France. With a colourful history linked to the Italian house of Savoy and the counts of Provence, it became popular with the English nobility on the Grand Tour. An English colony was established in the mid-18thC, and in 1849 they undertook to fund the famous Promenade des Anglais. It borders the sea for 4 km and has gardens, palm trees, beaches and exotic buildings such as the Negresco, a *belle époque* hotel-restaurant. Nice has much to offer, such as the high-quality entertainment of its festivals, art exhibitions, opera and events like the lenten carnival and battle of the flowers. The many museums make

Promenade des Anglais

Nice one of the cultural centres of France. A notable school of Niçois painting developed from 1450-1570 and its works can be seen in the Musée Masséna, Palais Lascaris and several churches. In the 1950-60s many young painters became well known, including Klein, Arman, Farhi and Malaval. Their works can be seen at the Musée d'Art Moderne et Contemporain. The *vieille ville* is a labyrinth of intriguing alleyways and shops, while the Roman settlement of Cimiez has baths, a small amphitheatre and a temple. The fish and flower markets are a blaze of colour and aroma, and *cuisine niçoise* is as good as the cooking anywhere else in France. Nice is an ideal place from which to make excursions by car, bus or train into the hinterland or by ferry to Corsica and the other nearby islands. Whether you stay in one of the many modest hotels or the opulent Negresco or Sofitel Splendid, you should allow two-three days to get to know the 'Queen of the Riviera'. See **NICE**.

Nightlife: The French Riviera is the most sophisticated area of the country outside Paris and has a plethora of casinos, nightclubs, piano bars and discos. All you need is energy and a steady flow of cash! See the **NIGHTLIFE** topic pages for **ANTIBES**, **CANNES**, **MONACO**, **NICE** and **ST. TROPEZ**, **Casinos**.

Opening Times:

Banks – 0900-1200, 1400-1600 Mon.-Fri. Busy central branches stay open at lunchtime.

Chemists – 0830-1200, 1400-1800 Mon.-Sat. A roster usually operates for Sun. opening.

Churches – In towns 0800-1800 but closed 1200-1400 in villages.

Currency exchanges (bureaux de change) – Times vary from 0830/0900/0930-1800/2200 Mon.-Sat.

Offices – 0830-1200, 1400-1800 Mon.-Sat.

Post offices – 0800-1900 Mon.-Fri., 0800-1200 Sat.

Restaurants – Usually 1200-1430, 1900-2200. Many close Mon. and some close for Aug. and a winter month.

Shops – Times vary enormously between 0800-1900, but smaller shops close for lunch 1200-1400. Others may close Mon.

Parc National du Mercantour: Incorporating La Vallée des Merveilles, this protected nature park of 70,000 hectares was established in 1979 and is adjacent to the Italian reserve of Argentara. Mountains, rivers and valleys contain chamois, marmots, ibex, wild sheep, flowers and butterflies. The northwest part of the park has mountains which rise to well over 2500 m, though the main ski resorts (see **A-Z**) are just outside its boundaries. In the Mont Bego (2873 m) area 100,000 rock engravings dating from the early Bronze Age have been discovered. From Menton drive via Sospel and Saorge to St. Dalmas-de-Tende and then to the village of Castorino to park beside Lac de Mesce. Les Merveilles Refuge offers board and lodging. No guns, dogs, radios, camping or fires are allowed. Information can be obtained from Direction du Parc National, 23 rue d'Italies, 06000 Nice, and professional guides can be hired from Alticoop, 3-4 rue Caroline, 06100 Nice, tel: 93985853.

Parking: In most towns parking meters operate between 0900 and 1900, although 1200-1400 is often free. The police and traffic wardens can impose fines and have illegally parked cars towed away. If impounded telephone the *mairie* (town hall) to reclaim your vehicle. See **Driving**.

Passports & Customs: A passport valid in Britain, Ireland or the EC allows the holder to stay for 90 days and no visa is required. Also acceptable are British visitors' passports and excursion passes, which can be obtained from post offices. If you wish to stay for more than 90 days, contact the local French police station (*commissariat de police*). Citizens from other countries, including the USA, Canada, Australia and New Zealand, require a visa which can be easily obtained from French embassies and consulates in those countries. See **Customs Allowances**.

Petrol: Petrol (*l'essence*) is available by the litre and prices are clearly marked in petrol stations (0800-2100), which are usually self-service. There are two grades: *super* and *essence*. Leaded petrol is *plomb*. See **Driving**.

Picasso, Pablo (1881-1973): The Spanish-born genius made his home in Vallauris, near Antibes, after World War II, and it was here that he developed his creative skill in ceramic design. In a disused scent factory he produced many paintings, sculptures and Madoura pottery, and inspired scores of local artisans. After ten years he moved to Cannes. Musée Picasso (see ANTIBES-ATTRACTIONS) in Château Grimaldi houses his ceramics, marine fantasia (a series of very strange 'marine'-style paintings), drawings and lithographs. The Musée Picasso (1000-1200, 1400-1800 Wed.-Mon.; 12F) in Vallauris has two major works, the painting *War and Peace* and a bronze statue of a man and sheep. He spent his final years in the farmhouse at Nôtre-Dame de Vie at Mougins (see **A-Z**).

Police: They can be recognized by their dark blue uniforms and flat caps. Always address them as Monsieur (or Madame) l'Agent: they are usually helpful to tourists. Any theft should be reported to the nearest police station (*commissariat de police*).
Main police stations:
Cannes: 93 Bd Alexandre III; Monaco: Pl. de la Visitation and Ave des Spélugues; Nice: Ave Félix Faure; Toulon: rue Xavier Savelli.
See **Crime & Theft**, **Emergency Numbers**.

Post Offices: Look for their yellow signs marked PTT or POSTES (postboxes are the same colour). They provide full postal services and telephones for both local and long-distance calls. These can be metered and paid for afterwards. Often a currency-exchange service is available. Postage stamps can be purchased from *tabacs*.

Main post offices:

Cannes: 22 rue Bivouac Napoléon; Monaco: Square Beaumarchais and Palais de la Scala; Nice: 23 Ave Thiers; Toulon: Pl. de la Liberté.

See **Opening Times**, **Telephones & Telegrams**.

Public Holidays: The following days are public holidays: 1 Jan.; Easter Mon.; 1 May; 8 May; Ascension Day (40 days after Easter); Whit Mon.; 14 July; 15 Aug.; 11 Nov.; 25 Dec.

Rabies: Still exists in France; as a precaution have all animal bites treated immediately by a doctor.

Railways: The French railway system is known as SNCF. One of the best ways of seeing the Riviera is by train, since the line runs close and parallel to the Mediterranean. Trains are frequent, punctual, clean and inexpensive. Remember to validate your ticket by punching (i.e. date-stamping) it in the machine before going on to the platform. Inspectors on the trains will fine non-validated ticket holders.

Two attractive excursions by train can be made into the hinterland from Nice. The Chemins de Fer de la Provence leaves from the second SNCF station, Gare de Sud, and goes to Digne, a town in an impressive mountain setting beside the river Bléone, 153 km northwest of Nice. The other, from the main SNCF station, goes to Cuneo/Coni in Italy via Breil-sur-Roya and Tende, 125 km northeast of Nice: don't forget to take your passport.

Main railway stations:

Antibes: Ave de la Libération, tel: 93995050; Cannes: 1 rue Jean Jaurès, tel: 93995050; Menton: rue de la Gare, tel: 93875050; Monaco: Ave Prince Pierre, tel: 93255454; Nice-Ville: Ave Thiers, tel: 93875050; Nice-Gare de Sud: 33 Ave Malausséna, tel: 93889488; Toulon: Bd P. Toesca, tel: 94915050.

L'Église Russe, Nice

Religious Services: France is predominantly a Roman Catholic country and details and times of services can be obtained from the town tourist office. There are Anglican churches in Nice, Menton, St. Raphaël and Monte-Carlo. See **Tourist Information**.

Renoir, Pierre Auguste (1841-1919): The great Impressionist painter spent his last 16 years at Cagnes-sur-Mer (see **A-Z**), in the villa Les Collettes, now the Musée Renoir du Souvenir. Musée Masséna (see **NICE-MUSEUMS 1**) contains five of his works.

St. Paul-de-Vence: Pop: 2000. 20 km west of Nice. Tourist information: rue Grande. This small, picturesque fortified hill village has attracted painters and artisans since the 1920s, including Bonnard, Signac (see **A-Z**) and Modigliani. Fondation Maeght (1000-1230, 1430-1800; 40F) is one of the best modern-art museums in France, built in 1964 with gardens, fountains, mosaics, sculptures and mobiles clustered round the pink and white building. It harbours paintings by Chagall (see **A-Z**), Braque (see **A-Z**), Miró, Kandinsky, Matisse (see **A-Z**) and Bonnard. Note though, that in midsummer the permanent collection gives way to temporary exhibitions. The Musée Provençal (1000-1200, 1400-1800; 22F) has displays on the town's history as well as armoury and sacred art, and is next to Église St. Paul-de-Vence, a 12thC church with a rich treasury. The village has many galleries, and antique and handicraft shops, and is often crowded with visitors. Recommended hotel-restaurants are Le Colombe d'Or, 1 Pl. du Général de Gaulle and Le St. Paul, 86 rue Grande, both of which are elegant and expensive. See **NICE-EXCURSION 1**.

St. Raphaël: Pop: 24,000. 43 km southwest of Cannes. Tourist information: Pl. de la Gare. A year-round fashionable resort on the bay of Fréjus with a fishing harbour, large marina, sheltered beach, fortified 12thC church, casino and Musée d'Archéologie Sous-Marine (1000-1200, 1400-1800 Wed.-Mon.; 10F), with displays on underwater archaeology. It is sedate – not as fast-paced as St. Tropez or Cannes – and a good choice for a family holiday. Recommended restaurants are La Voile d'Or, 1 Bd Général de Gaulle and Pastorel, 54 rue de la Liberté.

St. Paul-de-Vence

St. Tropez: Pop: 5500. 70 km east of Toulon. Tourist information: Quai Jean Jaurès. Originally a charming little fishing port, it became a centre for artists and writers (Signac – see **A-Z**, Bonnard, Matisse – see **A-Z**, and Colette), and from 1957 was transformed into the haunt of practically every film star after *And God Created Woman*, starring Bardot (see **A-Z**) and directed by Vadim, was filmed in the town. A marina, several beaches, the fine Musée de l'Annonciade, a 17thC fortress and fishermen's festivals known as *bravades* (see **Events**) contribute to its fame – even notoriety. However, the winter mistral blows fiercely and curtails the season, unlike that of any other Riviera resort. See **ST. TROPEZ**.

Shopping: All the towns featured have good shopping facilities. The larger superstores (*les grands surfaces*) tend to be situated outside town centres. They have a choice of food and wine to suit everyone's taste and pocket. Chic boutiques selling high fashion and jewellery abound in Monte-Carlo and Cannes. By contrast the many arts and crafts studios (*artisanat*) have a wide range of attractive and interesting *objets d'art*, usually at very reasonable prices. See NICE-SHOPPING, MONACO-SHOPPING, **Artisan Centres**, **Best Buys**, **Markets**.

Signac, Paul (1863-1935): A painter who used the pointillism technique created by Seurat, Signac lived at St. Tropez from 1892 onwards, in what was then a painter's paradise. A dozen of his works are in the Musée de l'Annonciade (see ST. TROPEZ-ATTRACTIONS).

Ski Resorts: In the French Maritime Alps, 60 km north of Nice, there are no less than 17 ski resorts, of which the best known are Auron, Isola 2000 and Valberg. They are a 2 hr drive along the N 202, which follows the river Var. Ask for the leaflet *Ski Azur* at Nice tourist office.

Smoking: Smoking is prohibited in museums, cinemas, theatres, churches and art galleries.

Sports: Spectator sports include grand prix car races at Monaco and Circuit Paul Ricard (Bandol), equestrian events, football, tennis tournaments, cycle races and, in every village, *pétanque* or *boules.*
Participatory sports:
Tennis: Every town has good-quality hard courts run by the municipal council, although private tennis clubs are located in Cannes, Antibes, Nice, Monte-Carlo and Toulon.
Cycling: See **Bicycle & Motorcycle Hire**.
Golf: Clubs can be found at Monte-Carlo, Cannes/Mandelieu, St. Raphaël/Valescure, Biot/Valbonne (13 km north of Cannes), Beauvallon (east of Grimaud) and Valcros (north of Bormes-les-Mimosas).
Swimming: In addition to the many Riviera beaches, most towns have large swimming pools (*piscines*) run by the local council. The beaches west of Antibes are sandy, and those east towards Italy shingle, although Monte-Carlo and Menton have 'imported' sand beaches. Some fashionable beaches in Cannes, Nice, Monte-Carlo and St. Tropez are 'private', i.e. hotel-owned.
Riding: There are riding facilities (*centres equestres*) in over 40 small towns and villages. Ask your local tourist office for details.
Fishing: Coastal fishing is unrestricted for non-commercial purposes. For inland river and lake fishing facilities, consult the local tourist office. You may need to join a local fishing club and pay a small fee. For the more adventurous the French Riviera also offers rock climbing, gliding, hang-gliding, rafting, canoe/kayak trips, sailing, potholing and walking (see **A-Z**). See **Water Sports**.

Taxis: Ranks are to be found at every SNCF station. Nice also has ranks at the airport, Acropolis, Promenade des Anglais, Pl. Masséna, Pl. Garibaldi and rue de l'Hôtel des Postes.
Taxi telephone numbers:
Antibes, tel: 93340347; Cannes, tel: 93383079; Menton, tel: 93284327; Monaco, tel: 93150101; Nice, tel: 93523232; St. Tropez, tel: 94970527; Toulon, tel: 94935151.

Cap d' Antibes

Telephones & Telegrams: You will find numerous payphones but the majority require a phonecard. Coin-operated machines take 1F, 5F and 10F coins. Phonecards (*télécartes*) are available from post offices and *tabacs* and cost 50F and 100F. To use a cardphone, lift the receiver, insert the card, pull down the handle above it and dial. For coin-operated telephones, insert the money first, then dial. In post offices (see **A-Z**) you can use a metered telephone which lets you make the call before paying. If using a café telephone you may have to buy a token (*jeton*) at the bar. Calls from your hotel room will be charged at a premium. Cheap rates are 2130-0800 Mon.-Fri., after 1400 Sat. and all day Sun. and public holidays. To telephone the UK from France dial 19, wait for the tone to change, dial 44 (11 for USA, 61 for Australia), then the STD number minus the first 0, then the number. To telephone France from the UK dial 01033 then the eight-figure provincial number. You can receive return calls at telephone booths. Telegrams can be sent from post offices or over the telephone by dialling 001111.

Television & Radio: There are six channels on French TV: TF1, A2, FR3, LA5, M6 and Canal + (the first paying and coded network). News broadcasts are at 0800, 1300, 2000 and 2300. French radio broadcasts in French on FM. It is possible to receive BBC Radio 4 by tuning to 1500 m on long wave, and 463 m on medium wave for BBC World Service. Radio Monte-Carlo has an English-language channel.

Time Difference: French standard time is GMT plus 1 hr, and the clocks go forward 1 hr in summer, making France 1 hr ahead of Britain apart from about four weeks in Oct. when the time is the same.

Tipping: A 15% service charge is included in your bill at all hotels and restaurants, as is TVA (VAT), so there is no need to leave anything unless you feel the service has been particularly good. If you pay by cash, any small change is usually left for the waiter. Hotel porters expect to receive approximately 10F per item of luggage, chamber-maids 10F per day, taxi drivers 10-15% of the fare and hairdressers about 10F.

Toilets: Public toilets are scarce, but all museums, restaurants, cafés, larger stores and railway and bus stations will have adequate facilities, signed 'Hommes' or 'Messieurs' and 'Dames'. You are expected to leave a small tip if there is a caretaker present.

Toulon: Pop: 182,000. 69 km west of St. Tropez. Tourist information: 8 Ave Colbert. Surrounded by high hills, the deep natural harbour makes Toulon the number one French naval port, as well as being an important and lively commercial city.
Although visitors on the Grand Tour came to Toulon in the 18th-19thC it had few cultural attractions. It was damaged in World War II (see **A-Z**) but the *vieille ville*, cathedral, two museums and harbour boat trips still warrant a visit. There are many hotels, including several in the inexpensive one-star category. Toulon is also well situated for excursions inland. See **TOULON**.

Tourist Information: Since the Riviera still attracts more tourists than any other region in France, there are efficient tourist offices, signified by a large 'I', in every town. They are usually to be found in the main street, or occasionally in the railway station, are open Mon.-Sat. and are always helpful with advice, maps and literature. They rarely change money but will advise on hotels (and may book for you if required), restaurants and local tours, and often arrange town visits. See **Accommodation**, **What's On**.

Transport: Local train and bus services along the coast are frequent, clean, inexpensive and run to time. Since the roads are usually crammed with traffic, in particular the corniches (see **A-Z**), you should consider the alternatives. The train trip from Nice to Menton takes you close to the sea, beaches and marinas, and is a relaxing way to sightsee. See **Airports**, **Buses**, **Railways**, **Taxis**.

Traveller's Cheques: See **Money**.

Vence: Pop: 14,000. 22 km west of Nice. Tourist information: Pl. du Grand Jardin. A pretty Roman market town surrounded by olive and orange trees, vineyards (St. Jeannet and La Gaude) and cultivated flowers. The town has been popular with writers and artists (it is 5 km from St. Paul-de-Vence – see **A-Z**), including Henri Matisse (see **A-Z** and D. H. Lawrence, and the *vieille ville* with its medieval ramparts and Romanesque cathedral is well worth a visit. Chapelle du Rosaire in Ave H. Matisse was designed by Matisse between 1947 and 1951. Although its exterior is like that of a house, inside the decoration is simple and predominantly white. Recommended restaurants in the town include La Rosaire and Domaine St. Martin, both on rte de Courségoules, and Les Portiques, 6 rue St. Veran. See **NICE-EXCURSION 1**.

Verdon, Grand Cañon du: Situated 40 km north-northwest of Draguignan, this is the longest (21 km), deepest (700 m) and most spectacular gorge in Europe, through which flows the river Verdon on its way westward to Provence. Look out, in particular, for Point Sublime, Balcons de la Mescla and Route des Crêtes. Cautious driving is advisable along the cliff-top roads. The best base from which to explore the area is Castellane, where Hôtel-Restaurant Ma Petite Auberge at 8 Bd de la République is recommended.

Villefranche-sur-Mer: Pop: 8000. 6 km east of Nice. Tourist information: Jardin François Binon. A lovely sheltered deep-water bay protects this small holiday resort and 17thC fishing port with Italianate-style houses coloured ochre or red, where Katherine Mansfield and Aldous Huxley once lived. The *vieille ville* with narrow alleyways, staircases, cafés and bistros has much charm. The 16thC Citadelle St. Elme houses two museums – Fondation Volti, displaying a local sculptor's work, and Musée Goetz-Boumeester, with works by two local painters, as well as Picasso (see **A-Z**) and Miró (both 1000-1200, 1500-1900 Wed.-Mon., Dec.-Oct.; free) – and overlooks the roadsteads called Darse and Rade, where cruise liners and NATO fleet warships lie at anchor. Two good restaurants are Le Massoury, Ave Léopold II and Mère Germaine, Quai Courbet. See **NICE-EXCURSION 2**.

Walking: The French take long-distance walking very seriously and the GRs (*grandes randonnées*) are well-marked trails which cross the region. The GR 51 runs parallel to the Mediterranean about 10-25 km inland. The GR 4 goes due north from Grasse, the GR 5 due north from Nice and the GR 52 due north from Menton. Many tourist offices organize summer excursions into the hinterland and mountains, for instance to Sospel, St. Étienne-de-Tinée, St. Martin-Vésubie and St. Laurent-du-Var. For more information, contact the Fédération Française de Randonnée Pedestre, 92 rue Clignancourt, 75007 Paris.

Water Sports: Sailing, windsurfing and water-skiing are available at all the major resorts and marinas (see **A–Z**), but particularly Île de Bendor, Île des Embiez, Port-Grimaud, Cannes and Monte-Carlo. Contact the Fédération Française de Voile, 55 Ave Kléber, 75084 Paris. For information about sailing schools contact the Centre d'Information Jeunesse Côte d'Azur, Esplanade des Victoires, 06000 Nice. For scuba-diving activities contact the Fédération de Sports Sous-marin, Fort Carré, 06600 Antibes. See **Sports**.

What's On: Tourist offices in Nice, Monte-Carlo and Cannes publish a monthly or seasonal guide to all local activities (in French). See **Events**, **Music**, **Tourist Information**.

Wines: There are a number of areas along the French Riviera which produce very drinkable wines. From west to east they are Le Castellet (10 km north of Bandol); Ollioules (7 km west of Toulon); St. Tropez; Bellet (3 km north of Nice); St. Jeannet and La Gaude (north of Cagnes-sur-Mer); and Menton. Most of these small regions produce red, dry white or rosé well suited to accompany *gigot* (lamb), *loup* (sea bass) or bouillabaisse.

World War II: The Riviera was occupied by the Nazis from 1942, when the French fleet of 60 ships was scuttled in Toulon harbour in Nov. of that year, although Mussolini had sent in his troops to occupy Menton in 1940. In Aug. 1944 American and French troops landed between Hyères and St. Raphaël, and 9000 paratroopers landed at Le

Muy near Draguignan on the 14th of the same month. Within two weeks the Riviera and Provence were liberated. The Memorial National du Débarquement (see **TOULON-ATTRACTIONS**) on Mont Faron overlooking Toulon commemorates these events. The American military cemetery near Draguignan (see **A-Z**) has the graves of 861 American soldiers of Gen. Patch's 7th Army, who were killed in the Liberation. Several towns and harbours including Toulon, Menton and St. Tropez were badly damaged by the Nazis before they were driven out.

Youth Hostels: For information consult the Centre d'Information Jeunesse Côte d'Azur, Esplanade des Victoires, 06000 Nice, tel: 93909393.

This book was produced using QuarkXPress™ and
Adobe Illustrator 88™ on Apple Macintosh™ com-
puters and output to separated film on a Linotronic™
300 Imagesetter

Text: Patrick Delaforce
Photography: Portfolios Photography
Electronic Cartography: Susan Harvey Design

First published 1992
Copyright © HarperCollins Publishers
Printed in Hong Kong
ISBN 0 00 435911-9